A GUIDE TO PRISONERS' RIGHTS
AND
PRISON LAW IN NORTHERN IRELAND

September 1998

Published by the Committee on the Administration of Justice
45/47 Donegall Street
Belfast BT1 2FG
Tel: (01232) 232394
Fax: (01232) 246706

Website:
http://ourworld.compuserve.com/**homepages/Comm_Admin_Justice/**

ISBN: 1 873285 78 7

Printed and bound in Belfast by
Shanway Distributors
461 Antrim Road
Belfast
BT15 3BJ

Cover design by Walter Steele, Belfast.

ACKNOWLEDGEMENTS

On behalf of CAJ, we would like to acknowledge the help and assistance of a large number of people who have assisted in the production of this Guide. Two US interns, Andy Cameron and Emily O'Connor, carried out sterling work on early drafting. Members of CAJ's Prisoners' Rights Subgroup including Martie Rafferty, Rose Perry, Lois Bickerstaff, Martin O'Brien, and Padraigin Drinan, read earlier drafts and provided useful comments and suggestions, as did other interested parties including Terry Perry. Thanks also to Lesley Emerson, Mike Ritchie, and Liz Martin (who was her usual indefatigable self), ably assisted by the equally unflappable Aideen Gilmore. We are also particularly grateful to Geoff Huggins of the Northern Ireland Prison Service who gave us invaluable assistance and advice in the latter stages of drafting as well as inordinate amounts of his time. To anyone else who has assisted with this Guide, many thanks.

The publication is supported by the European Union Peace and Reconciliation Programme through funding from the Northern Ireland Voluntary Trust.

Kieran McEvoy,

Chairperson,
**Committee on the
Administration of Justice**

Stephen Livingstone,

**CAJ Prisoners' Rights
Sub-group**

What is the CAJ?

The Committee on the Administration of Justice (CAJ) was established in 1981 and is an independent non-governmental organisation affiliated to the International Federation of Human Rights. CAJ takes no position on the constitutional status of Northern Ireland and is firmly opposed to the use of violence for political ends. Its membership is drawn from across the whole community.

The Committee seeks to ensure the highest standards in the administration of justice in Northern Ireland by ensuring that the government complies with its responsibilities in international human rights law. The CAJ works closely with other domestic and international human rights groups such as Amnesty International, the Lawyers Committee for Human Rights, and Human Rights Watch, and makes regular submissions to a number of United Nations' and European bodies established to protect human rights.

CAJ's activities include - publishing reports, conducting research, holding conferences, monitoring, campaigning locally and internationally, individual casework and providing legal advice. Its areas of work are extensive and include prisons, policing, emergency laws, the criminal justice system, the use of lethal force, children's rights, gender equality, racism, religious discrimination and advocacy for a Bill of Rights.

The organisation has been awarded several international human rights prizes, including the Reebok Human Rights Award and the Council of Europe Human Rights Prize.

For membership details and publications contact CAJ office.

TABLE OF CONTENTS

ANNEX A : PRISON RULES

ANNEX B : EUROPEAN CONVENTION ON HUMAN RIGHTS

ANNEX C : EUROPEAN PRISON RULES

ANNEX D : INFORMATION SHEET 21:
PRISONER ADJUDICATION PROCEDURES

ANNEX E : CASES CITED

INDEX

INTRODUCTION

This Guide is intended for prisoners and those who have an interest in their rights and welfare. It is intended to provide practical information on prisoners' rights, the duties of prison staff towards prisoners and how prisoners can make sure that their rights are respected.

The Guide does not consider every legal issue that might confront a prisoner, just those that present themselves as a consequence of imprisonment. For instance, the Guide gives information on obtaining legal advice and getting access to the courts to take a civil action such as divorce, but does not explain the law on divorce.

While focusing on the legal rights of prisoners the Guide also suggests informal action that may be a more appropriate way of pursuing some grievances. It is not always necessary to go to court to get a result.

Finally, although the Guide seeks to set out the general law as it applies to prisoners, some matters are dealt with briefly and the law will change. If in doubt always consult your legal adviser.

PRISONERS' RIGHTS

The basic position is:

> "Under English law a convicted prisoner, in spite of his imprisonment, retains all civil rights which are not taken away expressly or by necessary implication." (Lord Wilberforce, in *Raymond v Honey*, 1982)

This principle applies to female and male prisoners in Northern Ireland.

Imprisonment restricts the liberty of the individual and takes away some rights, but any other rights that are taken away must clearly be linked to the loss of liberty or expressly taken away under legislation. In recent years the Courts have set out prisoners' rights of access to the courts, correspondence and visits, association and freedom from arbitrary punishment.

In addition to prisoners' rights, prison staff have certain duties to prisoners such as to provide a safe and secure environment, to ensure safety in the work place and to offer access to proper medical treatment. Advice is given below on how you can take action to ensure these duties are complied with.

SOURCES OF PRISON LAW

The law as it affects prisons and prisoners is contained in primary and secondary legislation, international conventions and treaties and the decisions of the domestic and international courts. While there is some law that applies particularly to prisoners, other law applies to persons whether they are in custody or not.

Acts of Parliament

The key legislation in Northern Ireland is the **Prison Act (Northern Ireland) 1953** and the **Treatment of Offenders Act (Northern Ireland) 1968.** These acts provide for the management and operation of prisons and young offenders centres and give the Secretary of State the power to make prison rules.

Provisions relating to prisons and prisoners are contained in the **Northern Ireland (Sentences) Act 1998** and other criminal justice legislation such as the **Crime (Sentences) Act 1997,** which includes provisions relating to the transfer of prisoners between UK jurisdictions (this is considered below).

Other general legislation applies to prisons and prisoners, for example, the ordinary criminal law, health and safety at work legislation and food hygiene law. Legislation may be presumed to apply to prisons and prisoners unless it explicitly excludes them or if the powers, duties or rights are removed as a necessary consequence of a sentence of imprisonment.

Prison Rules

The **Prison Act** and the **Treatment of Offenders' Act** allow the Secretary of State for Northern Ireland to make rules for the management of prisons and young offenders centres. The most recent version of such rules are the **Prison and Young Offenders Centre Rules (Northern Ireland) 1995**.

The Prison Rules regulate much of the day-to-day life of prisons. They give governors and officers powers to manage prisoners, but also direct them how they should exercise those powers. Although the Rules do not confer legal rights (a prisoner may not sue prison authorities simply on the basis that the Prison Rules were not followed, *Becker v Home Office*, 1972) the courts will generally require prison staff to follow procedures and make decisions that respect the rules. A good example of this is the requirement that disciplinary charges should be laid within 48 hours of the discovery of an offence except in exceptional circumstances. The courts have quashed disciplinary awards where this requirement was not complied with.

Every prisoner has the right to consult the Prison Rules (Prison Rule 23(4)). In addition, a copy of the **Prison and Young Offenders Centre Rules (Northern Ireland) 1995** and recent amendments to the rules are included as **Annex A** of this Guide.

Standing Orders, Circular Instructions and Local Rules

Additional guidance to prison staff on procedures and processes is provided in the form of standing orders and circular instructions. Standing orders set out the general rules on correspondence, visits, privileges and a range of other matters. Circular instructions are used to provide instructions and guidance to governors on matters including temporary release, property, HIV and so on.

The governor may also make local rules. Any local rules must be in accordance with the relevant legislation including prison rules and standing orders.

Decisions of the Courts

Decisions of the courts lay down the law. Some decisions are interpretations of statutes or rules, in others the court will consider administrative processes or rights (such as access to the courts). Courts will generally follow their own previous decisions on an issue and there is a convention that lower courts will abide by the decisions of superior courts. In this Guide decisions of the Courts are given in *italics* with the year they were decided. Full citations are given in **Annex E**.

A major area of legal decision-making with reference to prisons is in judicial review. This follows from the requirement that decisions made by governors and officials are both within their powers and made in accordance with principles of natural justice. These decisions have clarified how governors and other staff should exercise their powers and the rights of prisoners to make representations and be given reasons for decisions that affect them. The procedures for taking judicial review are considered below.

As with legislation many non-prison cases have direct effect in prisons, for instance decisions relating to the law on negligence establish the nature of the duty of care that the Prison Service owes to prisoners.

International Conventions

There are a number of international instruments that have direct application to prisons. The two principal documents which have application in the United Kingdom are considered below. A third document, the **Convention on the Transfer of Sentenced Persons**, which deals with the repatriation of prisoners, is considered later.

European Convention on Human Rights: The European Convention on Human Rights (ECHR) sets out minimum standards for the protection of human rights within states, such as the United Kingdom, which have ratified the Convention. Although the Convention deals with general rights, a number of its articles have been relied on successfully by prisoners both in the United Kingdom and in other European jurisdictions. The development of prisoners' rights has been greatly assisted by the decisions of the European Court and Commission for Human Rights. The process of having a case considered by the court is extremely lengthy, however, the Government has introduced legislation, the Human Rights Bill, which will allow local courts to rule on alleged breaches of the Convention (this legislation will come into force during 1998). The European Court has decided cases in relation to correspondence and complaints processes which have had a direct impact on prison policy in the United Kingdom and elsewhere. A copy of the Convention is attached as **Annex B**.

European Prison Rules: The European Prison Rules set out minimum standards for the treatment of persons in custody. They are not mandatory, but signatories are encouraged to take action to bring their legislation into line with the terms of the European Rules. A copy of the European Prison Rules is included as **Annex C**.

ACCESS TO LEGAL ADVICE AND THE COURTS

Preparing Your Case

If you think you have a problem that might involve the law you should take the following steps:

- gather together all relevant documents;
- keep notes and copies of relevant communications;
- prepare and update a chronology of key events;
- prepare a list of witnesses or people with knowledge about the issues in the case;
- discuss the matter with friends; and
- consider contacting a solicitor.

Access to the Courts

Prisoners have a right to unimpeded access to the courts (*Raymond v Honey*, 1982). This means that the prison authorities may not prevent you from taking legal action in the courts and this includes the international courts.

Access to Legal Advice

Prisoners have a right to unimpeded access to solicitors for the purpose of receiving advice and assistance in connection with legal proceedings (*R v Home Secretary ex parte Anderson*, 1984; *Golder v UK*, 1975, *R v Secretary of State ex parte Leech*, 1993). However, access may be delayed for operational reasons such as a riot. Reasonable facilities for lawyers and prisoners to discuss legal matters must be provided at the prisons (Prison Rule 71).

Prisoners should not use telephones to discuss legal business as telephone conversations are monitored. A prisoner who uses the telephone to conduct legal business may have the privilege of telephone access withdrawn. It is permitted to use the telephone to arrange legal visits and make other practical arrangements.

Correspondence with lawyers and courts

Prisoners may write to their legal advisers or the courts regarding legal proceedings or other legal business. Such letters may not be stopped or opened unless the governor has reason to believe they contain material that is not related to legal proceedings (Prison Rule 72(4)). If the governor decides to open such correspondence he/she will generally do so in front of the prisoner and should read no more of the contents than is necessary to satisfy himself/herself as to its contents.

Prisoners must be provided with the writing materials necessary to correspond with their legal advisers and courts when they are party to legal proceedings. Any letters sent do not count against their entitlement to send letters.

Legal Visits

Prisoners may meet with their legal advisers to discuss legal proceedings which have already commenced or which are contemplated. Such visits do not require a permit and do not count against the prisoner's visiting entitlement, but 24 hours notice should be given to the prison. Prisoners do not have to disclose the nature of the legal proceedings and any legal visit will be held in the sight, but not the hearing of a prison officer (Prison Rule 71(1)). Prisoners may also be allowed a legal visit, with the permission of the Secretary of State, to discuss other legal business, such as making a will (Prison Rule 72(2)). Such visits will generally be permitted.

Legal Aid

Lack of money should not be a barrier to obtaining legal assistance. Legal aid is designed to provide free or subsidised legal advice on important matters to those who could not afford to pay for advice themselves. There are three basic schemes.

Criminal Legal Aid: This scheme provides funding for legal advice and representation for people charged with criminal offences. If legal aid is granted by the court all legal expenses will be paid under the scheme. In reaching its decision, the court will consider the seriousness of the offence charged and the ability of the alleged offender to pay for his or her legal defence.

Legal Advice & Assistance (Green Form Scheme): This scheme provides funding to allow people to obtain legal advice (except in relation to divorce and maintenance matters, landlord and tenant matters, and the drawing up of wills) and assistance in proceedings at tribunals (but not courts). Solicitors may give advice, write letters, take statements from witnesses, acquire a barrister's opinion, and prepare written case material for proceedings before tribunals. Legal fees may not run higher than £73.00 (at the time of writing). Eligibility is determined by the amount of income and savings of the client. The application form is green and should be filled out with the solicitor.

Legal Aid for Civil Court Proceedings: This scheme provides funding for work leading up to and including court proceedings. Eligibility is dependent upon income and savings and some clients may be asked to pay a portion of the legal fees. Application is made through the solicitor.

These schemes do not cover representation at and assistance regarding European Court proceedings. Legal aid in such instances is available through the Council of Europe.

Selecting a lawyer

The Law Society of Northern Ireland annually publishes a pamphlet listing the solicitors who participate in the legal aid schemes, the areas of law they practise, and their phone numbers and addresses. The pamphlet also contains more information about the legal aid schemes. For more information contact: Liaison Officer, Law Society of NI, Legal Aid Department; Bedford House; 16/22 Bedford Street; Belfast. Alternatively you can ask other prisoners if they know of a good solicitor.

Access to legal materials in prison

Access to legal materials in prison is limited. Within 24 hours of arriving at a prison every prisoner should be provided with information regarding the regulations and procedures of the prison (Prison Rule 23). The Prison Rules themselves may be consulted on request (Prison Rule 23(4)). Prison libraries may contain some legal materials but prisoners will usually have to rely on others to do more extensive legal research.

Discovery of documents

If a prisoner is party to legal proceedings (after papers have been filed with a court) they gain additional rights. In particular they may request that the court direct the Prison Service to grant access to documents in their possession which may be relevant to their case. This is called a discovery motion and will normally be made by a lawyer on behalf of the prisoner. Portions of prison files, transcripts from disciplinary hearings, medical reports, or more general policy documents and regulations may all be requested (*Williams v Home Office*, 1981). Courts, of course, may deny such discovery motions (*In re Hardy's Application*, 1988).

Petition for Habeas Corpus

A habeas corpus petition asks the court to issue a writ of *habeas corpus ad subjiciendum*. This writ orders the authorities to bring the prisoner before the court and legally justify their detention of the prisoner. If there is no legal justification for detention, the prisoner must be released.

Petition for habeas corpus is appropriate where prisoners are being detained for long periods of time without being charged or allowed court appearances, where prisoners are being held despite court orders to the contrary, or where the conditions of detention are so inhumane as to render the detention itself illegal.

The petition for habeas corpus is emergency in nature and receives priority over all others. The petition is made to the High Court and no outside parties need be served notice. If leave is granted, the petition is normally adjourned while notice is served on parties as the court directs.

CRIMINAL PROCEEDINGS

Bail Applications and Appeals where Bail has been refused

The idea of bail is that people accused but not convicted of criminal offences should not be held in prison unless absolutely necessary. Bail is an agreement between the defendant (or someone acting on his or her behalf) and the court that if released from custody the defendant will appear before the court on a specific day. Failure to appear is a criminal offence and will cause a sum of money (bond) to be forfeited to the court. Bail procedures differ depending upon the nature of the defendant's alleged offence. In granting bail a court may impose conditions on the defendant, for example, to reside at a particular address.

Bail in Non-Scheduled (Non-"terrorist") Cases: If a person is charged with a non-scheduled offence, bail will be decided by the Resident Magistrate (RM) at the first appearance in court. In deciding whether to grant bail, the RM will consider the gravity of the offence, the strength of the case against the defendant, the character and previous record of the defendant, the defendant's place of residence, and the likelihood that if released the defendant will commit an offence or tamper with court witnesses. If the RM refuses bail, the defendant may appeal to the High Court. If bail is refused the defendant must be brought back before the court every eight days.

Bail in ("Terrorist") Scheduled Cases: A defendant charged with an offence scheduled under the emergency legislation may only be granted bail by a High Court judge in Belfast, or a trial judge on the adjournment of the defendant's trial. If the judge thinks it likely that the defendant, if released, would abscond, commit an offence, or interfere with justice, bail is not to be granted. The judge must also consider the amount of time already spent in custody before making his/her decision. The emergency legislation requires the defence to argue the case for bail and in many cases bail is denied. If bail is refused the defendant must be brought back before the court every 28 days.

If bail is refused further bail applications may be made either at further remand hearings or at adjournments of the case. The court must consider each bail application afresh but it is unlikely that a previous ruling will be altered unless there has been a material change of circumstances.

Appeal against Conviction

A prisoner who has been convicted of a criminal offence and sentenced to a period of imprisonment may apply for the case to be considered on appeal and in scheduled cases has a right to an appeal.

Appeal from a Magistrate's Court: A prisoner may apply to appeal against the conviction (if he or she pleaded not guilty), the sentence, or both. Application to appeal must be made within 14 days. Notice of the defendant's intent to appeal must be sent within this time to the prosecuting attorney and the Clerk of the Court where the defendant was convicted. The appeal is to the County Court where there will be a complete rehearing of the case, without a jury. A greater or lesser sentence may be imposed by the County Court. In certain circumstances County Court decisions can be appealed to the Court of Appeal.

On appeal, the Court of Appeal will <u>not</u> reconsider factual questions decided by lower courts, only issues of law will be heard. Further appeal to the House of Lords (the highest court) requires the permission of the Court of Appeal. Only issues of law that are of great importance will be heard by the House of Lords.

Appeal from a Crown Court or Diplock Court

If convicted in a Crown Court a defendant may appeal the conviction on an issue of law without obtaining the permission of any court. Appealing the conviction on a point of fact requires the permission of either the Crown Court or Court of Appeal. Appealing the sentence requires the permission of the Court of Appeal. All appeals from the Crown Court are heard by the Court of Appeal.

If convicted in a Diplock court, a defendant may appeal his or her conviction or sentence without requiring permission as long as there had been a committal proceeding before the actual trial (Northern Ireland (Emergency Provisions) Act 1996). The appeal is to the Court of Appeal.

In any case the Court of Appeal may dismiss the appeal, allow the appeal and order a retrial, or allow the appeal and acquit the defendant. In dismissing an appeal, the court may increase or decrease the sentence handed down by the lower court. Appeals to the House of Lords are allowed only with the permission of the Court of Appeal or House of Lords.

CIVIL PROCEEDINGS

If a prisoner is assaulted, falsely imprisoned, or suffers injuries due to the negligent conduct of others, he or she may take action in civil court for damages against those responsible or their employers.

Assault

An assault is any act of physical contact with a person without that person's consent. To prove assault in a civil case it is necessary to demonstrate that there was no consent to the contact and that the contact was deliberate (or if the contact was unintentional that the person making the contact should have taken more care). The contact need not be aggressive and serious damage need not be proved in court. Spitting at a person or the cutting of their hair could count as assault. Governors and prison officers are given powers under the Prison Rules to perform activities that otherwise could be considered assaults. A clear example of such a power is the power to search a prisoner.

False Imprisonment

Prisoners may be falsely imprisoned if they are held in custody illegally or if the conditions of imprisonment fall below the minimum standards of treatment (*Meddleweek v Chief Constable of Merseyside*, 1985). The courts may require that prisoners prove that the intolerable conditions were imposed upon prisoners knowingly and wilfully by prison authorities (*R v Deputy Governor of Parkhurst Prison, ex parte Hague*, 1990).

Negligence

A claim for negligence may be made where a prisoner has been injured because of the failure of others to exercise reasonable care on their behalf. To succeed in an action for negligence a prisoner must show:

1. That the person (or organisation) being sued by the prisoner owed the prisoner a "duty of care". The Prison Service is responsible for the care and treatment of those held in its custody and so is required to take reasonable steps to provide a safe environment. In effect this means that in most cases the Prison Service owes prisoners a duty of care.

2. That the "standard of care" owed to the prisoner was not met. In any case where there is a duty of care the Court will consider whether the person being sued had taken reasonable steps to meet that duty. The Court will consider all circumstances of the case including the available staffing and administrative resources (*Porterfield v Home Office*, 1988). If the prison authorities had knowledge of a particular risk to prisoners they will generally be required to take steps to address that risk.

3. That the failure to take care caused the prisoner's injury. The court will consider whether the injury would have occurred anyway and if the harm or injury should have been anticipated by the prison authorities. If the court finds the injury would have occurred even if the duty and standard of care were met or that the injury could not have been anticipated a claim will fail.

In *Steele v NIO* (1989) a remand prisoner charged with sexual offences was assaulted by other prisoners. The court ruled that the authorities knew Steele to be at risk and could have done more to protect him. The absence of a policy to protect such prisoners was negligent on the part of prison authorities. Steele was awarded £6,000. Other successful actions have been taken for damage to prisoner's property or injuries suffered while bathing.

How to make a civil claim

You must make your claim within three years of the incident. If the claim is for less than £5,000, the action should be taken in the County Court, otherwise it should be taken in the High Court. There is a fee for making a civil claim in the courts (£55 in the County Court and £70 in the High Court).

Any civil action starts with the drawing up of a writ which sets out the nature of the case (this will usually be prepared by a solicitor). The writ must be served on the party being sued and the court where action will be taken. If the Northern Ireland Office or the Northern Ireland Prison Service is being sued, the writ should be served on the Crown Solicitor. The party being sued must respond to the writ with a 'notice for particulars'. The person making the claim will then file a statement of claim which details the case and the other party will prepare a document setting out their defence.

What You Can Win

If civil action is taken successfully monetary damages may be awarded. The damages that the court awards will depend upon the seriousness of the harm inflicted and are intended as compensation for loss or damage. In some cases the Court may award an additional 'punitive' amount if it finds that the conduct complained of involved an element of culpability.

Prisoners who have outstanding compensation awards against them in respect of their criminal convictions may lose all or some of any money awarded by the Court, which will be used to reduce the outstanding debt.

JUDICIAL REVIEW

Decisions and policies made by government officials (including prison officers and governors) must be in accordance with the law. An application for judicial review is a challenge to the lawfulness of a decision or policy and a request that the High Court take appropriate action to remedy the situation.

Grounds for judicial review

The High Court may intervene where it finds that the person making a decision or setting a policy:

- did not have the power to make the decision;
- in making the decision made an error in the interpretation of the law;
- in making the decision acted in breach of the principles of natural justice; or
- in making the decision arrived at a conclusion so unreasonable that no reasonable person in its position could have reached the same conclusion.

Application for judicial review

To apply for judicial review the prisoner must make an application to the High Court together with an affidavit (a sworn statement) which sets out the substance of the complaint. This application must generally be submitted within three months of the decision complained being made (although a judge may extend this period). Most applications for review are granted.

Judicial review hearing

If the application is accepted it will be heard by one High Court judge usually on the basis of sworn statements made by the prisoner and the government body whose decision has been challenged. Generally the prisoner will not be entitled to attend the hearing. If the judge rules against the prisoner the prisoner may appeal to the Court of Appeal.

Remedies

If the High Court grants judicial review it may order one or more of the following remedies:

a) certiorari: the decision is quashed (in most cases a further decision may be made);

b) prohibition: further action in relation to the matter is prohibited;

c) mandamus: a particular action is required (for instance the Court may direct that a decision be made);

d) injunction: an order not to act in a particular manner;

e) declaration: the Court makes a statement clarifying the legal position.

Monetary damages are generally only awarded if the prison authorities are shown to have acted in bad faith.

SMALL CLAIMS COURT

A prisoner who has an action for less than £500 against another person (not the Northern Ireland Office or the Prison Service) may file a claim with the Small Claims Court. Small claims courts specialize in arbitrating matters between individuals in an informal manner. For instance, a prisoner took action in the Small Claims Court against a local dry-cleaner who had damaged some of his clothing. Most actions heard by the Court are based on breach of contract or the sale of goods legislation. The Small Claims Court does not adjudicate on personal injury (negligence), libel or slander, legacy or annuity, ownership of land, property of marriage, or road traffic incidents.

Filing a claim

Filing a claim is fairly simple. Claim forms can be acquired from the Small Claims Court offices throughout Northern Ireland. Three copies of the form must be completed and sent to the claims office with the appropriate fee. The level of fees vary according to the size of the claim. The court will return one copy to the prisoner with the time, date, and place of the scheduled hearing. If the opposing party (the respondent) disputes the claim or counters with a claim of their own, the prisoner will receive notice to this effect. If the respondent does not dispute the prisoner's claim or does not respond to the court within 14 days of receiving the claim form the matter is considered undisputed and a judgment award will be made to the prisoner.

Hearing of the claim

If a hearing is necessary, the prisoner must attend unless told not to by the court. Prison authorities may let prisoners attend such hearings but may insist that prisoners pay for the transportation costs involved (which can be considerable if police escorts are required). Solicitors are permitted but are not necessary at the hearing and legal aid will not be granted. If the prisoner loses at the hearing the fee paid is lost. If the prisoner wins, he or she will receive a notification award in the mail stating the amount of the award. The person sued must pay the awarded amount in a reasonable time. If they fail to pay, the prisoner may seek payment through the Enforcement of Judgments Office within the Small Claims Court office. Prisoners who have outstanding compensation awards against them may lose all or some of any money awarded by the Court.

THE EUROPEAN COURT OF HUMAN RIGHTS

The European Court of Human Rights considers allegations that states have acted in breach of the European Convention on Human Rights. The United Kingdom ratified the Convention in 1953, and since 1965 individual citizens have been allowed to take cases to the Court. Legislation will come into force during 1998 that will make the Convention directly enforceable in courts in the United Kingdom. Even after this the Court will remain as an avenue if someone feels that domestic courts have not given effect to their Convention rights. Parliament and the courts will generally act in accordance with findings of the European Court.

Application to the Commission

In most cases prisoners must have taken action in the local courts before making an application under the Convention. The application, which is made to the European Commission for Human Rights, should be made within six months of the end of judicial or administrative proceedings in the United Kingdom. Application forms can be obtained directly from the Commission. Prisoners have an absolute right to write to and receive letters from the Commission and the Court.

Consideration of Admissibility

The Commission considers applications to identify whether they are admissible under the Convention. About 90% of applications are not accepted. If the Commission decides that a case is "admissible" it may refer it to the European Court. From October 1 1998 all applications should be made directly to the Court, which will take over the functions of the Commission with regard to deciding admissibility.

Commission's Opinion

The Commission will prepare a document setting out its view of the merits of the case which will be made available to the government, the prisoner and the Court. In most cases the Commission will also ask whether the parties can reach a 'friendly' settlement on the basis of its opinion and will allow a period for consideration.

Hearing before the Court

If no settlement can be agreed, the matter will be heard by the Court which will rule on the matter. Representation and legal preparation costs will be funded by the Court. The Court will consider the issues and rule on whether a breach of the Convention has occurred. The Court may also recommend that damages be awarded but has no power to compel payment.

Applicants should be prepared for long delays and only a slight chance of ultimate success.

INFORMAL METHODS OF AIRING GRIEVANCES

In addition to the legal options that prisoners have, there is also a range of formal and informal mechanisms to make requests or complaints. Prisoners are not required to use informal methods before taking legal action, but in many cases a quicker and more satisfactory result can be agreed.

Petition to governor

A prisoner may write to the governor or ask to see the governor to make a request. The governor is required to consider and provide a response to any request. The prisoner is not required to inform other staff of the subject-matter of any complaint. The governor should make time available on each day to see prisoners who request to see him or her, but s/he is not required to see a prisoner immediately.

Petition to Secretary of State

A prisoner may write to the Secretary of State in relation to any matter. A prisoner must be given a petition form on request. The petition should be completed by the prisoner making the request. Prisoners have the right to photocopy the completed form at their own expense. Prisoners may supplement the petition (through further petitions) until they receive a final reply. A reply to a petition will be sent to the governor for onward transmission to the prisoner. If necessary, replies will be read to prisoners outside of the presence of other prisoners. In practice replies are prepared by officials at Prison Service Headquarters acting on behalf of the Secretary of State. If the petition relates to matters which are the responsibility of the governor (and for which s/he will be required to provide the factual information for the answer) it will be passed to the governor for his/her comments.

In addition a prisoner may send a petition to the Secretary of State in a sealed envelope which will not be opened in the establishment. However, if the petition involves procedures or staff at the prison, the governor may be asked for his/her comments. A prisoner is entitled to a response in writing.

Request to see officer of Secretary of State

A prisoner may ask to see an officer of the Secretary of State (a civil servant from Prison Service Headquarters). The governor will make Headquarters staff aware of any such request when they visit the prison.

Application to the Board of Visitors

A prisoner may request to see a member of the Board of Visitors (or a member of the Visiting Committee at the Young Offenders Centre). The governor is required to make members of the Board aware of such requests when they visit the prison. Any interview may take place outside the sight and hearing of prison staff. The member will investigate the prisoner's request and report back to the prisoner.

Application to the Parliamentary Commissioner for Administration (Ombudsman)

If a prisoner considers that he or she has been the victim of maladministration (where administrative procedures - such as a review of security classification - have not been properly applied in his or her case, or are such as to prevent proper consideration of relevant issues) he or she can ask the Parliamentary Commissioner for Administration (PCA) to investigate. The PCA is only concerned with the procedures that are applied, not with the substance of the complaint. The PCA will prepare a report in respect of the procedures that have been challenged which the Prison Service is required to respond to in writing. The PCA does not have the power to quash or change a decision but may make recommendations which the Prison Service will probably follow.

Letter to MP or MEP

A prisoner may write to a Member of Parliament or a Member of the European Parliament to raise any issue of concern. In most cases the Member will write to the Prison Service or the Secretary of State to ask for comments before responding.

Letters to other interested organisations

In addition to raising issues through internal procedures and by writing to elected representatives, prisoners may write to groups such as the Northern Ireland Association for the Care and Resettlement of Offenders (NIACRO) or the Committee on the Administration of Justice (CAJ) for advice and assistance.

LIFE IN PRISON

Women Prisoners

In principle women prisoners are generally granted the same rights and privileges as their male counterparts, as well as a number of specified additionals. Under Rule 90(1) of the Prison and Young Offenders Rules (NI) 1995, women prisoners are entitled to be held separately from men. While Rule 91 (1) permits the governor to provide a regime with different work, education, recreation or privileges, Rule 91(2) specifies that this rule cannot be used for any discriminatory purpose which would otherwise be unlawful. In the past, however the prison authorities have in practice granted a less extensive range of prison privileges in certain areas such as education (e.g. a more restrictive range of educational and vocational classes). Such restrictions have been justified on the grounds of the considerably smaller numbers of women prisoners involved. Attempts at legal challenges to such differentials on the grounds that they were discriminatory have, to date, been unsuccessful, for example (*Spence v NIO* , 1993)

Health & Hygiene

While female prisoners' hair is trimmed if they so wish, like male prisoners, unless consent is given, a female prisoner will not have her hair cut shorter than the style worn on admission, unless the Medical Officer thinks it necessary for medical reasons. Toiletries may be purchased within the prison. Skin and hair products for particular use are not always available but these can usually be ordered. If a female prisoner has a skin condition which means that she must use particular creams, they can be prescribed by the Medical Officer.

Mothers and Children

Pregnant prisoners should, where possible, be removed to hospital for the period of their pregnancy and for the period thereafter which the medical officer deems appropriate. Maghaberry Prison has facilities for catering for prisoners who have a child. Whether or not a mother is permitted to have her child in prison is at the discretion of the Governor. The child is generally allowed to stay in the prison until it is 9 months old, but up to 14 months in exceptional cases.

Where children are in care, arrangements for visits are undertaken through the Social Services District responsible for the child. Provided that the social worker, Children's Home or foster parents consider a visit to the mother to be beneficial, this will be undertaken every three months. These arrangements will also apply in cases where children under 16 years of age are in hospital and are expected to remain there for three months or more.

Visiting Partners also in Prison

Visits between partners also in prison are permitted subject to security considerations. The initial visit between spouses should be allowed after both parties have spent 2 weeks in custody and thereafter will normally be allowed at one monthly intervals. Visits should last for the normal half hour period, although given that this is at the discretion of the Governor longer visits may be permitted. The current position is that if the partners are housed in the same prison (i.e. both are at Maghaberry) such visits will not count as part of the prisoners' normal entitlement so that the prisoner will not be required to issue a pass. If they are held at different prisons then normal visiting restrictions will apply.

Reception and Discharge

When a prisoner first arrives at prison he or she may be subject to the following actions:

- they may be searched;
- any property brought to the prison may be taken and held by the prison authorities during the period of imprisonment;
- they may be photographed, fingerprinted, palmprinted and measured;
- they may be asked to state his or her religious denomination (this is so that the appropriate chaplain may be identified and notified).

The prisoner should be interviewed by a governor shortly after arrival at the prison and seen by the medical officer within 48 hours of reception (during the committal process the prisoner will be interviewed by a nurse or hospital officer and may raise any immediate health needs at that time).

A prisoner should be given information about the prison's rules and regulations within 24 hours of reception and may consult the Prison Rules.

Before being discharged from prison the prisoner should be seen by a governor and the medical officer. Any property taken from the prisoner at reception must be returned to the prisoner. If clothes that were taken at reception have since been destroyed suitable clothing must be provided for the prisoner.

Privileges

The Governor is required to set up a system of privileges in each prison. Privileges may include newspapers, books, cell crafts, personal property, tuck shop, tobacco, parcels, telephones, television, radios and letters, visits and extra association.

Privileges should be generally available to all prisoners throughout the prison, however, the governor may restrict some privileges to prisoners who meet certain conditions such as time served or the fact that they have agreed to a conduct contract. In some areas it may not be possible to provide the full range of privileges (for instance, some parts of the prison estate do not have electric power points making in-cell television unavailable).

The governor may only withdraw privileges from an individual prisoner following proper disciplinary procedures and then only for a limited and specified period.

Safe Custody

The Prison Service has a duty to take reasonable care to provide prisoners with safe premises and a safe place and system of work (*Christofi v Home Office*, 1975; *Ferguson v Home Office*, 1977). The Prison Service should also take reasonable steps to protect prisoners from being assaulted by other prisoners or prison staff. If an attack on a prisoner is reasonably foreseeable the Prison Service should take action to protect that prisoner (*Egerton v Home Office*, 1978).

Searching

Prisoners may only be searched by prison staff in accordance with the prison rules (Prison Rule 16). There are two types of search a 'full search' (also referred to as a 'strip search') and a 'rub-down search'. Prison officers must use the minimum force necessary in conducting a search.

Full ("strip") search: If a prisoner has been outside the prison or in contact with visitors to the prison or if the governor has reason to believe the prisoner is in possession of a prohibited or unauthorised article which may only be discovered by a 'full search', he or she may be subject to a 'full search'. For a full search a prisoner is required to remove his or her clothing and will be subject to a visual examination by officers of the same sex. No other prisoners should be present during the search. Generally the procedure is that the prisoner will be required to remove clothing from the top half of their body which will be searched and replace that clothing before removing clothing from the lower part of the body. A full search does not allow body cavities to be examined, but a prisoner may be required to open his or her mouth.

Other searches: In circumstances in which the Prison Rules do not permit a full search a prisoner may be subject to a rub-down search for which he or she is not required to remove any item of clothing except for an overcoat.

If the rules on searching are not followed the search may be considered by a court to be unlawful and a prisoner may be successful in an action for assault.

Use of Force by Prison Staff

Prison staff may use force to maintain control and discipline in the prison, but only the amount of force necessary in the particular situation (Prison Rule 46).

Prison Classifications

A prisoner may be classified on the basis of his or her age, temperament, sentence length, conduct in prison or other relevant matters (Prison Rule 9). In Northern Ireland prisoners are classified as either 'star' or 'ordinary' class prisoners depending on whether they have previously been in custody. They may be re-classified on the basis of their conduct in prison. Star class prisoners are eligible for more pre-release leave but otherwise both classes are treated the same. A prisoner will be classified as a long-term prisoner if he or she is sentenced to 4 years or more in prison and as a short-term prisoner if the sentence is less.

Every prisoner will also be assigned a security categorisation based on their conduct in prison, the risk that they may escape and the risk to the public should they successfully escape. There are four security categories available at present - Top Risk (also known as 'Red Book'), High Risk, Medium Risk, and Low Risk. Most prisoners are either High or Medium Risk. In some prisons some facilities may only be available to prisoners in the lower security categories.

The prison authorities must act fairly in deciding a prisoner's classification. If a prisoner considers that his or her classification is not fair, s/he may ask for the decision to be reconsidered and may also seek judicial review of the decision.

Correspondence

Prisoners may write to friends and family and to other persons or organisations. However, a person may ask the Prison Service to stop future correspondence from a prisoner. The governor may also stop correspondence between a prisoner and a person or an organisation if s/he has reason to believe that the person or organisation concerned is planning or engaged in criminal activities or other activities which would present a genuine and serious risk to the security or good order of the prison. Correspondence between prisoners (unless they are close family) may be subject to restrictions.

Statutory letters: a prisoner is entitled to send and receive a letter immediately following his or her reception into prison and to send and receive a letter each week he or she is in custody (Prison Rule 68). This is a right and may not be taken away. The postage for the letter will be paid by the Prison Service.

Privilege letters: a prisoner may send a second letter each week which will be paid for by the Prison Service.

This is a privilege and may be taken away as a disciplinary punishment. The governor may allow prisoners to send further letters at their own expense.

Letter in place of a visit: a prisoner may send a further letter paid for by the Prison Service in place of a visit.

Correspondence with lawyers and courts: see above.

Correspondence with MPs: prisoners may correspond with Members of Parliament and with Members of the European Parliament subject to the normal conditions of correspondence.

Censorship: the Prison Service may read any letter (with the exception of privileged legal correspondence) entering or leaving the prison. Prisoners can generally write on any subject but correspondence may not contain:

- anything likely to encourage violence;
- escape plans or material that would jeopardise the security of a prison;
- plans or materials which would tend to assist or encourage the commission of any disciplinary offence or criminal offence;
- material which would jeopardise national security;
- descriptions of the making of any weapon, explosive, poison or other destructive device;
- obscure or coded messages which are not readily intelligible or decipherable;
- threats of violence or of damage to property likely to induce fear in the recipient;
- blackmail or extortion;
- material unlawful by reason of its indecency or obscenity;

- information which would create a clear threat or present danger of violence or physical harm to any person;

- complaints made on behalf of other prisoners;

- material which is intended for publication or for use by radio or television (or which, if sent, would be likely to be published or broadcast) if it: (i) is for publication in return for payment (unless a prisoner is unconvicted); (ii) is likely to appear in a publication associated with a person or organisation to whom the prisoner may not write; (iii) is about the prisoner's own crime or past offences or those of others, except where it consists of serious representations about conviction or sentence or forms part of serious comment about crime, the processes of justice or the penal system; (iv) refers to individual prisoners or members of staff in such a way that they might be identified; (v) is in contravention of any of the other restrictions on content applying to letters.

- in the case of a convicted prisoner, material constituting the conduct of a business activity; provided that for these purposes business activity does not include: (i) the conferment of a power of attorney or the making of other arrangements for a person outside prison to conduct a business activity on the prisoner's behalf; (ii) the winding up of a business by a newly convicted prisoner; (iii) the sale, transfer or other disposal of the prisoner's personal property, or the transfer of his/her personal funds; (iv) other personal financial transactions provided that in a 12-month period such transactions do not, in relation to any convicted prisoner, exceed the current limits on the amounts which may be spent by employed male or employed female prisoners, as the case may be, from private cash within the prison.

- in the case of a prisoner against whom a deportation order is in force, material constituting or arranging any financial transaction unless the Governor is satisfied that there is a real need for such a transaction (e.g. the support of near relatives or the seeking of advice to petition against deportation). This restriction does not apply to a prisoner whose sentence includes a recommendation for deportation but in respect of whom a decision has not been made by the Home Secretary to act upon the recommendation.

- in the case of a prisoner in respect of whom a receiving order has been made or who is an undischarged bankrupt, material constituting or arranging any financial transaction except: (i) on the advice of the Official Liquidator or the Official Assignee for Bankruptcy; (ii) to pay wholly or in part a fine or debt in order to secure the prisoner's earlier release; (iii) to defend criminal proceedings brought against the prisoner; (iv) to meet the cost of communicating with or instructing a solicitor to act upon the prisoner's behalf in bankruptcy proceedings.

Any letter entering or leaving the prison which breaches these rules may be stopped. If an outgoing letter is stopped the prisoner should be informed and given a chance to rewrite the letter.

Language: a prisoner may correspond in any language, but letters not written in English may be subject to delay.

Letters that contain unlawful material: letters may be turned over to the police if prison authorities believe the contents are unlawful or contain information regarding a criminal offence.

Visits

Prisoners may be visited by friends and family and by other persons with the agreement of the governor or Secretary of State. Usually three adult visitors are allowed per visit, but the governor may permit more on request. Children must be accompanied by an adult.

Statutory visits: a prisoner is entitled to receive a visit once in every period of 4 weeks (Prison Rule 68). This is a right and may not be taken away.

Privilege visits: 3 extra visits per month may be allowed by governors as privileges. These visits may be taken away as punishments for disciplinary offences.

Duration of visits: visits should usually be at least thirty minutes long.

Prisoners subject to cellular confinement: prisoners in cellular confinement as a disciplinary punishment are entitled to their statutory visits and (unless they have been removed as part of the punishment) their privilege visits. However, the governor may defer visits until the end of the period of cellular confinement. If the governor does so the prisoner may take the deferred visits in addition to his/her normal visiting entitlement later.

Visiting conditions: all non-legal visits will normally take place in the sight and hearing of prison officers. Visitors are not allowed to bring in cameras or other recording devices but they may make notes. However, any notes may only be removed from the prison with the agreement of the governor.

Irish Language

Prisoners may correspond in Irish and are allowed access to a wide range of publications in Irish. However, materials in Irish may be delayed leaving or entering the prison to allow Prison

Service staff to examine them.

The governor may require that visits take place in English.

Participating in Elections

While imprisoned, convicted prisoners cannot vote in Westminster elections (Representation of the People Act 1983, s3(1)). Remand prisoners may vote in all elections. Convicted prisoners serving more than a one year sentence cannot be members of the House of Commons while serving their sentences (Representation of the People Act 1983, s1).

Discrimination

Prisoners retain rights to equal treatment while in prison and may not be discriminated against on the grounds of their sex, religion, race or political beliefs.

Prisoners may rely on the Sex Discrimination Order 1976, the Race Relations Order of 1997 and the Constitution Act 1974 each of which protect specific rights to equal treatment

Medical Treatment

Access to health care. All prisoners should be examined by a medical officer on reception (Prison Rule 21(1)). The medical officer should see prisoners who complain of illness daily (Prison Rule 86(4)) and see prisoners immediately who are reported to be seriously ill (Prison Rule 86(5)). S/he should also visit any prisoner under restraint or in cellular confinement every day (Prison Rule 86(8)). If the medical officer believes that a prisoner requires treatment in an outside hospital he should recommend this to the governor. Untried prisoners have the right to be visited by a doctor or dentist of their choice, provided they are willing to pay the cost and the governor considers such a visit is reasonable (Prison Rule 104(3)). Convicted prisoners only have access to a doctor of their choice when the examination is in connection with legal proceedings (Prison Rule 72(5)).

Prisoners should also have access to dental and optical care (and most costs are met by the Prison Service).

Confidentiality. Prisoners are entitled to the same standard of medical confidentiality as people outside prison. They may have access to their medical file under the same arrangements as members of the public and doctor/patient confidentiality may only be broken where this is necessary for ensuring the safety of a third party (*W v Edgell,* 1990).

Standards of health care. Prisoners are entitled to the same standard of care within a prison as they would expect outside. The standard test for medical negligence, whether the doctor has acted in accordance with what would be accepted as proper by a responsible body of medical practitioners skilled in that particular art, also applies to medical care in prison.

Consent. The same rules apply to prisoners as to everyone else. They may not be subject to medical treatment without their consent. Courts have indicated that prisoners who decide to refuse food or fluids may not be treated without their consent if they are aware of their situation and retain a capacity to make a decision.(*ex parte Robb,* 1995)

Mental health. Prisoners who are suffering from mental health problems should consult the medical officer who may refer the prisoner to the prison psychiatrist. In some cases the prisoners may be transferred to the prison hospital or to Maghaberry for observation or treatment. In certain circumstances a prisoner may be transferred to an outside hospital.

Hygiene

Every prisoner must be provided with toilet articles necessary for health and cleanliness. These articles must be replaced as necessary. Prisoners must be allowed to shave every day and take a hot bath or shower at least once every week. Washing and bathing facilities must meet the requirements of the Health and Safety at Work legislation.

Exercise and association

If prisoners are not engaged in outdoor work, they must be allowed at least one hour of outdoor exercise every day (weather permitting). Prisoners who have been segregated as punishment retain normal exercise privileges unless otherwise specified.

Clothing

Prisoners are entitled to wear their own clothes in prison, but some types of clothing are prohibited (for example, "hand wash" labelled clothing, articles that look like prison officers' clothing, and articles of clothing that have sectarian associations). If a prisoner does not wish to wear his or her own clothing, clothing must be provided by the prison. Prisoners may wear a mixture of private and official issue clothing items. Prisoners may not swap clothing.

Food

Food served by the prisons must be wholesome, nutritious, and well-prepared (Prison Rule 82(1)) and the medical officer should regularly sample prison food (Prison Rule 82(5)). Prisoners should inform the prison medical officer of any special dietary requirements they have. Prisoners must be over 16 years of age to smoke cigarettes.

Parcels and Money

A prisoner may receive a weekly parcel from his or her family or friends as a privilege. Parcels may contain clothes, food (mostly fruit), confectionery, tobacco, and toiletries. The quantities permitted are limited by the Prison Service. Special parcels may be allowed at Christmas, Easter, and Halloween.

If a parcel or sum of money for a prisoner is received at a prison, the prisoner must be told how it is dealt with by prison officials. If money is received, prison officials may credit the sum to the prisoner's account, return the money to the sender, or, if the sender's address is unknown, use their discretion as to how to dispose of the money. If the money has been sent on behalf of a prisoner who has been committed to prison for default of payment of a fine, the money may only be used to pay the fine with the prisoner's agreement.

Books, Newspapers and Periodicals

As a privilege prisoners may receive books, newspapers, or periodicals while in prison (subject to the requirements of security and the local rules that apply with regard to the number of items that may be received). Prisoners may receive such items from family members or visitors or by subscription. Normally, prisoners are allowed to keep a reasonable number of these materials in their cells. Newspapers are provided by the governor for prisoners in association.

Reading material may be withheld as punishment, but any material that arrives at the prison during the time that a prisoner has lost privileges should be held until the privilege is restored. Prisoners receiving more than three days of cellular confinement as punishment are allowed access to newspapers at public expense. There are no restrictions on the language of materials coming into the prison, but materials are subject to censorship and if they are in a language other than English may be subject to delay. Any restriction of access to information about current affairs must be compatible with Article 10 of the European Convention on Human Rights.

Prisoners may request notebooks and/or drawing books and such requests should normally be granted. Subject to the normal rules on correspondence (see above) prisoners may send out of the prison completed notebooks or other artistic or written material.

Library

Each prison must have a library and prisoners should be allowed to borrow books or other materials (Prison Rule 54).

Education

The Prison Service is required to offer a range of educational classes for prisoners and to allow prisoners to attend classes to the extent practicable (Prison Rule 52). Facilities should also be made available for prisoners who wish to engage in correspondence courses or private study (Prison Rule 52(3)). Educational materials that are sent to the prison are subject to the same rules as correspondence.

Religion

Prisoners have the right to practise their religion to the extent compatible with good order and discipline (Prison Rule 56) and may have in their possession religious books or other materials necessary for that purpose (Prison Rule 64). Chaplains for the main Christian denominations are appointed for each prison. The religious denomination of a prisoner is recorded when s/he is received at the prison (Prison Rule 57) and the chaplain for that denomination is required to visit each prisoner recorded for his/her denomination (Prison Rule 59). If a prisoner belongs to a religious denomination for which no chaplain has been appointed, the governor should do what he or she reasonably can to arrange for a visiting chaplain if the prisoner desires it.

Prisoners are not required to work on recognized days of religious observance (Prison Rule 51(8)) .

Business Activity

A prisoner may not engage in business activities while in prison, but should be allowed reasonable facilities for arranging such conduct on his or her behalf. The governor has the discretion to allow prisoners to deal with a limited range of business matters (e.g. disposal of property, signing cheques, making a will).

Marriage

Prisoners have the right to marry while in prison. The denial of this right was found to be a violation of Article 12 of the European Convention (*Hamer v UK*, 1982).

DISCIPLINARY PROCEDURES

General

Prison disciplinary proceedings are intended to support good order and discipline in the prison. Although the governor has powers to punish prisoners who break the rules those powers must be exercised fairly. Disciplinary procedures are subject to judicial review and if a Court finds that procedures have been breached or applied unfairly it may quash a governor's decision.

The Prison Service provides an Information Sheet on adjudication procedures which is attached as **Annex D**.

Disciplinary Offences

A prisoner may only be charged with an offence under Prison Rule 38. If the offence is criminal the governor may request that the police investigate it.

Before the Adjudication

The charge must be laid within 48 hours of the discovery of the offence except in exceptional circumstances (Prison Rule 35(1)). To allow the prisoner to prepare his or her defence, the prisoner:

- should receive a copy of Information Sheet 21 together with a statement of the charge;

- may request to see a copy of all statements to be submitted in evidence and be informed of the names of any witnesses to the incident in advance of the hearing (*R v Board of Visitors, HM Prison Blundeston, ex parte Fox-Taylor,* 1982);

- may try to consult a solicitor before the adjudication (if there is not sufficient time or a solicitor is not available, the governor hearing the adjudication will decide if it is necessary for the hearing to be adjourned to allow for a consultation),

If the offence is of a serious nature the governor may refer the charge to the Secretary of State. In most cases the Secretary of State will delegate his/her authority to conduct the adjudication to the Board of Visitors or Visiting Committee. If the charge is to be heard by members of the Board of Visitors or the Visiting Committee the prisoner will be informed.

Segregation before the Adjudication

A prisoner charged with a disciplinary offence may be held separately for up to 48 hours before the adjudication if the governor considers it necessary (Prison Rule 35(4)). However, segregation must be justified in each case (*In re Hunter's Application*, 1989).

The Adjudication Procedure

The adjudication must take place on the day after the charge is laid unless that day is a Saturday, Sunday, public holiday or a day of religious observance (Prison Rule 36(2)). Throughout the adjudication the governor is responsible for ensuring that the prisoner understands what is going on and that the process is conducted in a fair and open manner.

The procedure at the adjudication is as follows.

1. The governor will begin by ensuring that the prisoner understands the charge and has had an adequate opportunity to prepare his/her defence.
2. The governor will ask if the prisoner wants legal representation or other assistance - if the prisoner makes a request the governor must consider the request and make a decision.
3. The governor will ask the prisoner whether he or she pleads guilty or not guilty and ask if he or she wants to call witnesses.

4. The reporting officer will give his or her evidence and the prisoner will have the opportunity to ask questions. If there are other witnesses they will give their evidence and the prisoner will be allowed to question them.

5. If the prisoner has pleaded guilty he or she may make a verbal statement including any factors he or she wishes to be taken into consideration by the adjudicator in reaching a finding.

6. If the prisoner has pleaded not guilty he or she may now make his or her defence. An oral statement can be made or a written statement can be read and the prisoner may comment on the evidence given.

7. The prisoner may also ask to call witnesses. It is for the governor to decide if a witness should be allowed, but he or she should only refuse to call a witness if he or she considers that they will not give evidence that will assist in establishing exactly what happened. The prisoner may question the witnesses on any relevant matter and they may also be questioned by others present including the reporting officer.

8. The prisoner may make a further statement after the evidence has been heard.

9. Having heard all the evidence the adjudicator will announce the findings on each charge.

10. If the prisoner is found guilty the adjudicator will ask if there is anything that he or she wishes to say in support of a request for leniency before any punishment is imposed. A prisoner may also ask to call someone to speak on his or her behalf. The adjudicator may ask for a report on the prisoner's conduct in custody to be given and the prisoner

should be allowed to ask questions in connection with that report.

11. The adjudicator will then announce the award(s) for any offence(s) proved and should explain the award if necessary.

The governor or Board of Visitors may only award a punishment from the list set out in the prison rules and must provide a written record of the punishment awarded (Prison Rules 39-43).

Legal Representation

Prisoners do not have a right to be represented at disciplinary hearings. If legal representation is requested it is for the governors or Board of Visitors to decide taking into account the following factors (*R v Home Secretary, ex parte Tarrant*, 1984):

1. The seriousness of the charge and the potential punishment.
2. The difficulty of the legal issues involved.
3. The ability of the particular prisoner to prepare and present a defence to the charge.
4. Any procedural difficulties involved in the case.
5. The need for reasonable speed in conducting adjudications.
6. The need for fairness in conducting the adjudication.

If a request for legal representation is made at the start of the adjudication or during the adjudication the governor or Board of Visitors must consider the request and make a decision before continuing.

In practice most requests for representation are refused and most refusals are upheld by the courts. However, if refused the prisoner may request an adjournment to consider his/her defence or to request legal advice from a solicitor and this request must also be considered. If legal representation is granted, the hearing should be adjourned until a legal adviser has been appointed.

Fairness in Adjudications

Disciplinary hearings are not intended to be courts of law and need not adopt all the procedural safeguards of the courts (*In re O'Hare's Application*, 1988). Disciplinary hearings in front of governors, in particular, "should be exercised with great expedition" and are "necessarily fairly crisp hearing[s]" (*Hone v Board of Visitors, HM Prison Maze*, 1988; *In re Crockard's Application*, 1985). Nevertheless, natural justice requires that the procedures in disciplinary hearings should be fair in all circumstances (*R v Board of Visitors, HM Prison Hull, ex parte St Germain (No 2)*, 1979). Based on these principles, the courts have made the following rulings:

- the prisoner must have a written statement of the charge;

- the prisoner must have an opportunity to present his or her case (Prison Rule 36(4));

- the charge must be proved beyond reasonable doubt;

- prisoners can call witnesses if their testimony will be relevant (*In re Stephenson's Application*, 1987);

- the governor cannot compel a witness to testify at a disciplinary hearing (*In re Quinn's Application*, 1988);

- prisoners have the right to question witnesses that have testified against them (*In re Quinn's Application*, 1988);

- prisoners do not have an absolute right to see statements made against them (which are not presented as evidence) but such statements should be made available to them where they contradict other evidence (*R v Board of Visitors, HM Prison Gartree, ex parte Mealy*, 1981);

- the formal rules of evidence do not apply, but hearsay evidence should be treated carefully (*In re Duffin's Application*, 1988; *R v Board of Visitors, HM Prison Hull, ex parte St Germain (No 2)*, 1979);

- if two charges stem from one incident or set of facts, the prisoner may not be given a punishment for each charge (*In re Murphy's Application*, 1988).

At the proceedings prisoners may make notes. In addition the governor is required to keep a record of the adjudication, including information about the charge, the evidence presented and any decisions made during the adjudication (such as to refuse legal representation) (Prison Rule 36(7)).

Review of Decisions

If the prisoner considers that he or she has not been treated fairly, or that the punishment is more severe than it should be, he or she may petition the Secretary of State and request that the finding of the adjudication be quashed or the punishment mitigated (Prison Rule 45).

A prisoner may also apply for judicial review of an adjudication (see above).

SEGREGATION & RESTRAINT

Prisoners have a general right to associate with other prisoners. Association may include meals, work, exercise, education and other activities. Prisoners may be excluded from association only under the following circumstances.

Restriction of Association

Prisoners may have their association restricted, either generally or for particular purposes, if the governor considers it is necessary for good order or discipline, or if it is in the prisoner's own interests (Prison Rule 32). The governor may not restrict association in this way for more than 48 hours without the agreement of a member of the Board of Visitors or the Secretary of State. If the Board of Visitors or the Secretary of State agree to an extension that extension may not exceed one month. The governor should give the prisoner reasons for the use of this power and the restriction should not be any greater than necessary. This power may not be used as a punishment.

Cellular Confinement

Cellular confinement may be imposed as a punishment if a prisoner is found guilty of a disciplinary offence. The governor may award up to 3 days cellular confinement (Prison Rule 39(1)(f)) and the Board of Visitors or Secretary of State may award up to 56 days (Prison Rule 40(2)(f)). The governor must visit a prisoner undergoing cellular confinement once a day (Prison Rule 41(3)). Before a punishment of cellular confinement may be imposed the medical officer must say that the prisoner is fit to undergo the punishment (Prison Rule 41(2)).

Prisoners only lose privileges which have been removed as part of a disciplinary award or are necessarily removed as a consequence of cellular confinement. So while a prisoner will lose privileges that require association, privileges that he or she can enjoy in his or her own cell (such as reading) are only lost if specifically removed.

Segregation Pending Adjudication

A prisoner who is charged with an offence against discipline may be kept apart from other prisoners until the disciplinary hearing takes place. This should not be done routinely, however, and the governor must use his or her discretion reasonably in each case.

Temporary Confinement

A prisoner may be temporarily segregated in order to prevent disturbance, damage or injury (Prison Rule 39). Temporary confinement of refractory or violent prisoners may be in special cells or protected rooms. This power may not be used as punishment, and segregation under the rule must terminate when the prisoner has ceased to be refractory or violent. The medical officer must be informed of such prisoners and has the power to order temporary confinement. Both the governor and medical officer must visit prisoners temporarily confined once a day. A prison officer must observe these prisoners every 15 minutes and keep records of the observation.

The Use of Restraining Devices

Restraints may only be employed where they are necessary to prevent prisoners from injuring themselves or others, from damaging property, from creating a disturbance, or to insure safe custody during transfer (Prison Rule 48). The governor must consult with the medical officer as soon as possible after issuing such an order. Notice of a restraining order must be given to a member of the Board of Visitors. Restraining devices should be used for no longer than is necessary and never for more than 24 hours without the written agreement of a member of the Board of Visitors.

REMAND PRISONERS

Remand prisoners are prisoners who have not been convicted of an offence, or who have been convicted and are waiting to be sentenced. Because they are technically innocent in the eyes of the law, they are allowed additional privileges in prison and possess more rights. The treatment of remand prisoners should be such as to reflect "their status as persons who have not been convicted of any offence" (Prison Rule 97(2)).

Prison Life

Remand prisoners must, as far as is reasonable, be kept out of contact with convicted prisoners (Prison Rule 99). They may not be photographed or measured without the authority of the Secretary of State (Prison Rule 98) and they may not be required to work (Prison Rule 103(3)).

Contact with the Outside World

Remand prisoners may receive one parcel every week and may send and receive as many letters as they wish (subject to the practical considerations of the prison) (Prison Rule 101). Postage on two letters a week will be paid for by the Prison Service. Correspondence is subject to the same rules regarding content as for other prisoners (see above). Remand prisoners have the right to have as many visitors as they wish, although in practice they are limited to three visits per week. Visits may also be restricted during holiday periods (*In re Mulvenna's Application*, 1985).

TRANSFER AND REPATRIATION

Transfer

Convicted prisoners may apply to transfer between jurisdictions within the United Kingdom under the Crime (Sentences) Act 1997. Generally a transfer will be permitted if the prisoner has family links in the jurisdiction that he or she wishes to transfer to and if the prisoner has at least six months of a sentence to serve. There are two type of transfer - restricted transfer and unrestricted transfer.

Unrestricted transfer: If a prisoner is granted an unrestricted transfer he or she is treated as if they had been sentenced by the courts in the jurisdiction to which they are transferred. All matters in relation to release are dealt with according to the laws and rules in that jurisdiction.

Restricted transfer: If a prisoner is granted a restricted transfer the sending jurisdiction retains responsibility for some aspects of the prisoner's sentence, including in all such cases, the arrangements for ultimate release. Most other matters, including temporary release (except for prisoners transferred for time-limited periods to receive accumulated visits) are dealt with under local rules.

Prisoners will usually not be permitted an unrestricted transfer if the effect of such a transfer would be to reduce significantly the period they are required to serve in custody. In practice, this makes it more difficult for prisoners transferring to Northern Ireland to be granted an unrestricted transfer as the remission and other release arrangements are more generous than in the other United Kingdom jurisdictions.

Repatriation

Prisoners may apply to be repatriated from Northern Ireland to countries outside the United Kingdom to serve their sentences

(Repatriation of Prisoners Act 1984; Convention for the Transfer of Sentenced Persons).

The Northern Ireland Prison Service is required by the Council of Europe to provide information on request to sentenced prisoners who may be eligible to apply to be repatriated to their home country to serve their sentences. Prisoners may make an application for repatriation to the authorities in Northern Ireland or they may apply direct to the authorities in the country that they wish to be transferred to. In either case the agreement of the authorities in both countries and of the prisoner is required before any repatriation takes place.

A prisoner is required to be a national of the state to which s/he wishes to be transferred. However, many states will interpret this test quite widely. Repatriation is possible between many European countries, some Commonwealth countries, the United States, and some other countries. Only sentenced prisoners may be repatriated and prisoners will not be repatriated if there are proceedings pending against them or if they have outstanding appeals.

Following repatriation the prisoner's sentence will be administered under the laws that apply in the jurisdiction to which he or she is repatriated. The prisoner must be given a written explanation of what this means in practice before giving their agreement to the terms of the repatriation. The authorities in the United Kingdom will generally not grant a repatriation where it would result in the prisoner serving a shorter period in custody, but this is unlikely to affect prisoners sentenced in Northern Ireland as the remission arrangements are more generous than elsewhere (and as a consequence prisoners will generally be required to serve longer in custody if repatriated from Northern Ireland).

RELEASE FROM PRISON

Life Sentence and Secretary of State's Pleasure Prisoners

Life is the mandatory sentence for murder and the maximum sentence for some more serious crimes (attempted murder, manslaughter, and the most serious firearm and sexual offences). Prisoners convicted of a murder committed while under the age of 18 years are required to be detained at the Secretary of State's Pleasure (SOSP).

The Secretary of State makes release decisions for life sentence and SOSP prisoners and sets the general policy for the review of life sentences by the Life Sentence Review Board (LSRB) which provides advice to the Secretary of State in relation to individual cases. The LSRB is an internal administrative body composed of officials and some professionals (forensic psychiatrists and the Chief Probation Officer). The Governors of Maze and Maghaberry attend as advisers and will discuss the outcome of the board with the prisoner afterwards.

Life sentence cases are reviewed at the three and six year points of sentence by the Life Sentence Unit at the Northern Ireland Office. The purpose of these internal reviews is to identify whether there are particular mitigating factors that would suggest that the case should be considered for the first time by the LSRB earlier than normal. However, most cases are considered by the LSRB at the 10 year point in sentence (at the 8 year point for SOSPs).

Life sentence prisoners in Northern Ireland are required to serve a period in custody that reflects the seriousness of the particular offence committed by the prisoner. In addition, consideration will also be given to the need to deter others from committing similar offences in the future and the risk that the particular offender may commit further serious offences if released.

Prisoners convicted of offences of a similar nature (for instance, drivers involved in a murder) will generally serve a similar period in custody in the absence of particular risk issues, but much depends on the particular circumstances of the offence.

Before the LSRB considers a prisoner's case the prisoner will be interviewed by prison governors who will write reports for the Board. The prisoner has access to all papers provided to the Board with the exception of those reports for which a Public Interest Immunity Certificate is claimed (in practice, professional reports and governor's reports). The prisoner will be given information about cases that the Board will consider as 'comparators' (that is cases which have previously been considered by the LSRB that have features that make them relevant to the consideration of his or her case). The prisoner may make representations to the Board or others may make representations on his or her behalf. In addition, with the agreement of the prisoner, a probation officer may prepare a report on the prisoner.

The Board considers each case at a formal meeting. Neither prisoners nor their representatives may attend the hearing. If the Board decides to recommend release to the Secretary of State the prisoner will be informed of that recommendation and given a provisional release date. The views of the judiciary will also be requested. The Secretary of State will then make a decision in relation to release. If the Board does not recommend release it will set a date for the next review of the prisoner's case. The maximum period that a prisoner's case will be 'knocked back' is three years. All reviews after the first are conducted by the LSRB. In addition to being informed of the date of the next review, a prisoner who is not recommended for release will also be given a written statement explaining why the Board has not recommended him for release. This statement is not a full account of the Board's consideration of the case, but is intended to give the prisoner the 'gist' of the consideration. If new issues arise in relation to a prisoner's case between review, the prisoner may request that the date of the next review be brought forward and that request will be considered.

Prisoners who are recommended for release are generally required to participate in a pre-release scheme. This scheme is designed to integrate the prisoner into the community over a period of time and is composed of stages of temporary release which increase in duration over a period of time. In the final stage the prisoner lives and works in the community and is only required to report to a prison fortnightly. The period on the pre-release scheme, normally 9 months, counts as part of the period in custody in setting the provisional release date.

Because of the nature of their sentences (which are effectively 'for life'), life sentence prisoners and SOSPs are released on licence and remain on licence until they die. They may be recalled at any time by the Secretary of State. However, in practice the policy that has been applied in Northern Ireland is that prisoners will only be recalled if they are considered to pose a serious risk to public safety. In some cases, particular licence conditions may be set. (See also the Northern Ireland (Sentences) Act 1998 discussed below).

Remission for fixed sentence prisoners

Prisoners serving fixed sentences are entitled to remission (a discount) of their sentence. Prisoners may only lose remission as a disciplinary punishment in accordance with the general rules on adjudications (see above). Prisoners may not have their sentence reduced to less than five days by remission.

The general remission rate is set under Prison Rule 30 as up to half of sentence, but prisoners sentenced to five years or more for a scheduled offence committed after 31 March 1989 may not receive more than one third remission of sentence (Northern Ireland (Emergency Provisions) Act 1996 s.15). However, under the Northern Ireland (Remission of Sentences) Act 1995 these prisoners may be released on licence after serving half their sentence. The licence continues to the two-thirds point of sentence. Should the prisoner be reconvicted after release the judge may require that the unexpired part of the sentence be served. (See also the Northern Ireland (Sentences) Act 1998 discussed below).

Temporary Release

Prisoners in Northern Ireland may apply for temporary release from prison under a range of schemes. The main schemes are pre-release temporary release, Christmas home leave, the 10-day allowance, and compassionate temporary release. The criteria for these schemes vary from time to time and prisoners should ask the prison for further information on these schemes and on other forms of temporary release.

The main schemes are as follows:

- **Christmas Home Leave:** available to prisoners who have served more than a given period in custody (currently 10 years), prisoners who are eligible for pre-release leave and prisoners in their last year of sentence; at present prisoners receive 10 days leave. In the case of life sentence prisoners their case must have been considered by the LSRB before they become eligible for home leave;

- **10-day allowance:** available to prisoners who have served more than a given period in custody (currently 10 years), at present prisoners receive 10 days that they can take at any time during the year. A similar requirement to have been heard by the LSRB applies;

- **Compassionate temporary release:** available to prisoners to allow them to visit seriously ill close relatives (parents, grandparents, children,

> grandchildren, brothers and sisters, husbands and wives) or to attend funerals;

- **Pre-release temporary release:** available to prisoners to help them re-integrate into society prior to release; prisoners are allowed a series of temporary releases during the latter stages of sentence; more leave is granted to prisoners serving longer sentences; prisoners serving longer sentences may begin to take the leave a longer period before release (up to two years in some cases).

The Prison Service will consider each application for temporary release taking into account the purpose of the application and other factors including the risk of re-offending. In making decisions the Prison Service must act fairly, and temporary release decisions are subject to judicial review.

Early Release under Northern Ireland (Sentences) Act 1998

As a result of the **Northern Ireland (Sentences) Act 1998** prisoners convicted of scheduled offences are entitled to apply for early release. This section sets out the qualifying criteria and procedure for seeking release.

Qualifying Criteria

To seek early release a prisoner must satisfy the following criteria

- Serving a sentence passed in Northern Ireland for a scheduled offence committed before 10 April 1998, which was not descheduled by a certificate of the Attorney General. If the prisoner was transferred from England, Scotland or Wales the offence must be equivalent to a scheduled offence. Transferred prisoners can seek certification from the Attorney General in England and

Wales or the Lord Advocate in Scotland that their offence is an equivalent offence

- The sentence must be one of life, or imprisonment for at least 5 years

- The prisoner must not be a supporter of a terrorist organisation. These are defined by an order of the Secretary of State. The Secretary of State may by an Order add to or remove organisations from this list.

- The Sentence Review Commissioners must be satisfied that if released immediately the prisoner is not likely to become a supporter of a terrorist organisation or to become involved in acts of terrorism connected with the affairs of Northern Ireland

- If a life sentence prisoner, the Sentence Review Commissioners must be satisfied that if released immediately the prisoner is not likely to be a danger to the public.

Application Procedure

Prisoners can apply to the Sentence Review Commissioners, which is a body of people appointed by the Secretary of State. A panel of three Commissioners will make a preliminary indication as to whether they are minded to accept the application or not, and in the latter case why not.

This indication is then sent to the applicant and the NIO and, if it is accepted by both, it is confirmed immediately in a substantive determination. However, if either party challenge the preliminary indication then that indication is set aside and an oral hearing, at which the applicant prisoner and the NIO may be present and represented, will be convened. After the hearing the Panel will make a final determination, which can only subsequently be challenged in very limited circumstances.

Generally the only course open to either the applicant or the NIO at this stage is to apply to the courts for judicial review of the decision.

Any hearing in relation to the application will normally be held in private. A prisoner may apply for legal aid in respect of any representation before the Commissioners and can apply to call witnesses if they think this is relevant. The rules may permit some proceedings to be conducted in the absence of the prisoner or their representative but if so the Attorney General may appoint a person to represent the prisoners interests in those proceedings. Evidence given in the course of these proceedings will not be admissible in respect of criminal proceedings relating to membership of a proscribed organisation. On receipt of a request from a victim of an offence, or a member of their family, the Secretary of State may provide information about whether a person has made an application for release and what its outcome was. However, the Secretary of State shall not provide such information where he or she believes that it would create a danger to the safety of any person.

If Release is Granted

If the Commissioners decide to grant release then

- If the prisoner is serving a **FIXED TERM** they should be released on the day after they have served **one third** of their sentence plus one day for every day of remission lost and not restored under the Prison Rules.

- If the prisoner is serving a **LIFE SENTENCE** then the Commissioners must specify a day which marks the end of **two thirds** of the time the person would have been likely to spend in prison. The prisoner is entitled to be released the day after that date.

- Whatever release date is set a prisoner is entitled to *accelerated release* if the date falls two years after the Act comes into force (for prisoners sentenced before the Act came into force or who were in custody awaiting trial before it came into force) or two years after the sentence began for those sentenced after the Act came into force. The accelerated release day will then be either two years after the Act comes into force or two years after the sentence began.

- All prisoners shall be released on licence. The licence conditions are that they will not support a terrorist organsiation or become involved in acts of terrorism. In addition in the case of a **LIFE SENTENCE** prisoner that they do not become a danger to the public. This licence may be suspended by the Secretary of State if they feel the person concerned has broken or is likely to break the licence conditions. Where a licence is suspended the case will be referred to the Sentence Review Commissioners who will decide whether to confirm or revoke the licence.

If Release is Refused

The Commissioners must give notice of their decisions and the reasons for it to the prisoner and the Secretary of State. Rules made under the legislation may indicate whether and in what circumstances future applications may be made.

RIGHTS FOLLOWING RELEASE

Access to Benefits

Remand and convicted prisoners are not entitled to receive Income Support or Unemployment Benefit while in prison. They may continue to collect Child Benefit, One Parent Benefit or Guardian's Allowance. Benefits may be available for home leave and upon release.

Prisoners on remand who do not receive a sentence or a suspended sentence of imprisonment are entitled to receive some benefits that are suspended for any period that was spent in custody. If a remand prisoner is not convicted, or is convicted but not given a sentence or suspended sentence, he or she is entitled to the benefit payments that would have been collected during the remand period. Remand prisoners should contact DHSS for more details.

Employment

If a prisoner was employed prior to being sent to prison (on remand or following conviction) in some circumstances he or she may be entitled to re-instatement (or compensation) following release. In most cases the period of imprisonment will be such as to end the employment relationship between the prisoner and his or her previous employer, but an employer must consider the length of time the prisoner was employed and imprisoned, the position the prisoner held, and the importance of quickly getting a replacement for that particular position (*Hare v Murphy Bros.*,1974; *F.C. Shepherd & Co. v Jerrom*, 1987).

Rights Lost by Conviction

Convicted prisoners sentenced to five or more years are permanently disqualified from serving on juries. Those sentenced to between three months and five years are disqualified from jury service for ten years from the date of their release (Juries (NI) Order 1974 s.1(1) and (2)).

Convicted prisoners sentenced to three or more years are permanently prohibited from possessing firearms or ammunition. Those sentenced to between three months and three years are prohibited for five years from the date of their release (Firearms Act 1968 s.21(1), as amended by s.14 of the Criminal Justice Act 1982). These prohibitions are in addition to any general restrictions under the criminal law.

Disclosure of Convictions

Following release from prison a prisoner may be required to inform a prospective employer in making an application for employment that he or she had been convicted of a criminal offence. Similar information may have to be provided in other circumstances. However, prisoners who have been sentenced to two and a half years or less are not required to disclose convictions after a period of time has elapsed (Rehabilitation of Offenders Order (Northern Ireland) 1978). There are exceptions, such as if the released prisoner were to apply to join the police or to work with children as well as applications for certain licenses, for instance, for firearms. The periods before a conviction is 'spent' are - if the sentence was more than two and half years the conviction is never spent; if the sentence was more than 6 months and two and a half years or less, the conviction is spent after 10 years (five years if under 17 at the time of conviction); and if the sentence was six months or less than seven years (3 years if under 17 at time of conviction).

Registration of Sex Offenders

Prisoners convicted of certain sexual offences are required to register with the police following release (Sex Offenders Act 1997). They are required to register within 14 days and to provide information including their name, any aliases they use, their date of birth and their home (or main) address. The Prison Service will generally inform prisoners who are required to register of the requirements of the law, but the responsibility for registering lies with the prisoner. Failure to register is a criminal offence.

Assistance Upon Release

Convicted prisoners who were sentenced to seven days or more and who have not participated in work-out schemes will receive a discharge grant upon release. The prisoner must apply in order to receive this grant. Prisoners should contact the probation department well in advance to ensure prompt payment. All prisoners should receive travel vouchers to enable them to get home on the day of their release. Some prisoners may be entitled to Income Support or unemployment benefits after release.

INFORMATION FOR FAMILY AND FRIENDS

Visiting Prisoners

A visit begins with a permit sent by the prisoner to the visitor. Visitors must bring the permit to the prison. They also should bring some formal form of identification which has the same address that is found on the visit permit.

A prison officer or civilian searcher may ask to search a visitor to a prison, but has no right to do so. However, if a prisoner refuses to agree to a search the officer may refuse to allow the visitor entry to the prison (Prison Rule 49). Any search must be by and in the presence of officers of the same sex as the visitor. Visitors' valuables will be taken and sealed before they are taken to the visiting area. Generally all a visitor is allowed to bring in to the visiting area are some cigarettes, money, and perhaps a bottle and nappy for a baby. Children under 16 should be accompanied by an adult. Money can be signed in for a prisoner.

A governor may suspend any visit if there are reasonable grounds for suspecting that anyone visiting is bringing in or taking out any improper article, or that the purpose of the visit may subvert discipline or good order.

Transport to the Prison

Transportation to and from prisons can be difficult to arrange and expensive to take. Information regarding visits and transportation, as well as letters, social welfare issues, housing, and so on can be obtained by calling Prison Link, a service organization run jointly by the Probation Board for Northern Ireland and NIACRO.

Probation Board can also be contacted by families of prisoners, and families can request to meet with probation staff members for advice.

Financial assistance for some visits is available for visitors in receipt of welfare benefits. Payments are made by DHSS through local social security offices. Close relatives who meet financial qualifications may claim two visits every four weeks up to a maximum of 26 visits a year. Assistance for emergency visits is also available. Those who qualify will receive payment for return fare to the prison by the cheapest route possible. If visitors are unable to return the same day the cost of meals and overnight accommodation may also be covered. In addition, the costs for taking dependant children should be met. To apply for assistance, go to the local social security office and ask for explanatory leaflet PV11 and application form PV9. Bring with you the visit permit that you received from the prison. Claims and payments should be processed in advance of visits.

Assistance for Family Members of Prisoners

A prisoner's family may be eligible for welfare benefits under the normal rules applying to applicants. NIACRO and other welfare organisations can provide detailed advice.

ANNEXES

ANNEX A - PRISON RULES

Prison and Young Offenders Centre Rules (Northern Ireland) 1995, Prison and Young Offenders Centre (Amendment) Rules (Northern Ireland) 1995, Prison and Young Offenders Centre (Amendment) Rules (Northern Ireland) 1997.

1995   No. 264

PRISON AND YOUNG OFFENDERS CENTRES

The Prison and Young Offenders Centre (Amendment) Rules (Northern Ireland) 1995

Made   22nd June 1995

Coming into operation   1st August 1995

To be laid before Parliament

The Secretary of State in pursuance of section 13 of the Prison Act 1953(a), as extended by section 2 of the Treatment of Offenders Act (Northern Ireland) Act 1968(b), hereby makes the following rules-

Citation and commencement

1.   These rules may be cited as the Prison and Young Offenders Centre (Amendment) Rules (Northern Ireland) 1995 and shall come into operation on 1st August 1995.

Interpretation

2.   In these rules any reference to the principal rules is a reference to the prison and Young Offenders Centre Rules (Northern Ireland) 1995(c).

Inquiry into change

3.   (1) In paragraph (3) of Rule 36 of the principal rules the words "pending further investigation" shall be omitted.

     (2) Paragraph (5) of that rule should be omitted.

71

Disciplinary awards

4. In paragraph (2) of Rule 95 of the principal rules after the word 'one' insert 'or more' and in paragraph (4) substitute for the words 'rule 92' the words 'rule 94'.

Revocation

5. The Prison Rules (Northern Ireland) 1983(a) and the Young Offenders Centre Rules (Northern Ireland) 1983(b) are hereby revoked.

Northern Ireland Office	P.B.B. Mayhew
22nd June 1995	One of her Majesty's Principal Secretaries of State

EXPLANATORY NOTE

These rules amend the Prison and Young Offenders Centre Rules (Northern Ireland) 1995 (the principal rules)

Rule 3 amends Rule 36 of the principal rules to extend the circumstances in which the governor may adjourn a disciplinary adjudication.

Rule 4 amends Rule 95 of the principal rules. The inclusion of the phrase 'or more' enables a governor to award more than one punishment where a young offender has committed a disciplinary offence. The rule also replaces the incorrect reference to Rule 92 in the principal rules.

Rule 5 repeals the Prison Rules (Northern Ireland) 1983 and the Young Offenders Centre Rules (Northern Ireland) 1983 which were not repealed by the principal rules.

1995   No 86

PRISON AND YOUNG OFFENDERS CENTRE

The Prison and Young Offenders Centre (Amendment) Rules (Northern Ireland) 1997

Made   20th February 1997

Coming into operation   1st April 1997

To be laid before Parliament

The Secretary of State in pursuance of section 13 of the Prison Act (Northern Ireland) 1953(a), as extended by section 2 of the Treatment of Offenders Act (Northern Ireland) 1968(b), hereby makes the following rules:

Citation and commencement

1.   These rules may be cited as the Prison and Young Offenders Centre (Amendment) Rules (Northern Ireland) 1997 and shall come into operation on 1st April 1997.

Interpretation

2.   In these rules any reference to the 'principal rules' is a reference to the Prison and Young Offenders Centre (Northern Ireland) 1995(c).

General Principles

3.   In paragraph (1)(f) of Rule 2 of the principal rules after the word 'sex' insert the word 'religion'.

Temporary release

4.   In Rule 27 of the principal rules add:

"(5) In considering any application for temporary release under this rule previous applications, including any fraudulent applications, may be taken into account".

Offences against prison discipline

5.   After paragraph (11) of Rule 38 of the principal rules insert:

"(11b) provides false information in an application for temporary release."

Police interviews

6.   In paragraph (1) of Rule 69 of the principal rules after the word 'prisoner' insert the words 'willing to see him'.

Northern Ireland Office	P.B.B. Mayhew
20th February 1997	One of Her Majesty's Principal Secretaries of State

EXPLANATORY NOTE

(This note is not part of the Rules)

These Rules amend the Prison and Young Offenders Centre Rules (Northern Ireland) 1995 (the principal rules).

Rule 3 amends Rule 2 of the principal rules to include religion in the list of criteria that may not be used in allocating facilities and privileges.

Rule 4 amends Rule 27 of the principal rules to allow previous applications for temporary release, including fraudulent applications, to be taken into account in considering applications for temporary release.

Rule 5 amends Rule 38 of the principal rules to create a new disciplinary offence of providing false information in an application for temporary release.

Rule 6 amends Rule 69 of the principal rules to require the consent of a prisoner to a police interview under the rules.

STATUTORY RULES OF NORTHERN IRELAND

1995, N0. 8

PRISONS AND YOUNG OFFENDERS CENTRES

The Prison and Young Offenders Centre Rules (Northern Ireland) 1995
Made.......................   10th January 1995

Coming into operation..............   1st March 1995

To be laid before Parliament

PRISONS AND YOUNG OFFENDERS CENTRES RULES (NORTHERN IRELAND) 1995

TABLE OF CONTENTS

PART IV

DISCIPLNE AND CONTROL

PART IX
PHYSICAL WELFARE

PART X
WOMEN PRISONERS

PART XI
PERSONS ORDERED TO BE DETAINED IN A YOUNG OFFENDERS CENTRE

PART XII

UNTRIED PRISONERS

PART XIII

PRISONERS COMMITTED FOR COMTEMPT ETC.

PART XIV

GENERAL RULES RELATING TO OFFICERS

Committee on the Administration of Justice

PART XV

SPECIAL RULES RELATING TO GOVERNORS

PART XVI

POWERS AND DUTIES OF BOARDS OF VISITORS

SCHEDULE

Prisons

The Secretary of State in pursuance of section 13 of the Prison Act (Northern Ireland) 1953 (a)[1] as intended by section 2 of the Treatment of Offenders Act (Northern Ireland) 1968 (b)[2], hereby makes the following rules-

---

[1] 1953 c. 18 (N.I.) as modified by S.I. 1973/2163 (1973 III, p. 7541)

[2] 1968 c. 29 (N.I.) as modified by S.I. 1973/2163

PART I

PRELIMINARY

Citation and commencement

1. These rules may be cited as the Prison and Young Offenders Centre Rules (Northern Ireland) 1995 and shall come into operation on 1st March 1995.

General principles

2. (1) These rules are made with regard to the following general principles-

> (a) All prisoners committed by the courts shall be held safely and securely for the protection of the community and in the interests of justice;

> (b) The treatment of prisoners shall be such as to sustain their self-respect and health and to encourage them to develop a sense of personal responsibility;

> (c) Prisoners' living conditions shall be compatible with human dignity and acceptable standards in the community;

> (d) Prisoners will be offered opportunities to use their time constructively while in prison and will be encouraged to do so;

> (e) Each prisoner will be considered individually and where appropriate will be able to contribute to decisions regarding how he spends his time while in prison;

> (f) Facilities and privileges shall be made available to prisoners, individually or as members of a class without discrimination on the basis of race, colour, sex, language, political opinion, national or other origin, birth, economic or other status;

(g) Where a decision is taken which affects the conditions of imprisonment of a prisoner, or a class of prisoners, the reasons for that decision will be made available;

(h) Order and discipline in prison shall be maintained at all times with firmness and fairness but with no more restriction than is necessary for safe custody and well-ordered community life;

(i) Prisoners shall be given facilities to maintain links with their families and encouraged to do so and assisted in other respects to prepare themselves for eventual release;

(j) Prisoners retain all rights and privileges except those removed as a necessary consequence of their imprisonment;

(k) Information will be made available to prisoners to enable them to understand the prison regime and to make use of the facilities available under it.

(2) These principles, taken together, are intended as a guide to the interpretation and application of the rules.

Application

3.   (1) These rules shall apply to all prisoners held in lawful custody.

(2) The rules shall apply to women prisoners subject to Part X.

(3) The rules shall apply to inmates held in a young offenders centre subject to Part XI.

(4) The rules shall apply to untried prisoners subject to Part XII.

(5) The rules shall apply to prisoners committed for contempt or otherwise lawfully detained without conviction subject to Part XIII.

Interpretation

4. (1) In these rules -

"the Act" means the Prison Act (Northern Ireland) 1953;

"board of visitors" means a board of visitors appointed for a prison under section 10 of the Act;

"centre" means a young offenders centre provided under section 2(a) of the Treatment of Offenders Act (Northern Ireland) 1968;

"chaplain" means a minister of any religious denomination appointed under section 9(1) of the Act;

"chief medical officer" means the chief medical officer of the Department of Health and Social Services;

"code of conduct" means any code of conduct approved by the Secretary of State under rule 6;

"foreign national" does not include a citizen of the Republic of Ireland;

"the governor" means the governing governor of a prison whether or not present at the prison;

"a governor" means any governor and includes an officer acting with authority under rule 117(2) or rule 117(3);

"inmate" means a person required to be detained in a young offenders centre;

"legal adviser" means, in relation to a prisoner, the prisoner's counsel or solicitor and includes an accredited clerk acting on behalf of a solicitor;

"medical officer" means the officer, being a registered medical practitioner, appointed by the Secretary of State to perform the functions of that officer;

"officer" means an officer of a prison;

"prisoner" means any person required to be detained in a prison;

"privilege" means any of the privileges under rule 10;

"public holiday" means any holiday which is published by means of a Circular Instruction made by the Secretary of State and includes bank and privilege holidays;

"visiting committee" means the committee appointed by the Secretary of State under section 3 of the Treatment of Offenders Act (Northern Ireland) 1968.

Prisons

5.   (1) The Secretary of State may, in pursuance of section 1 of the Act:-

(a) declare that any premises, building, enclosure or place shall be a prison;

(b) alter the boundaries of any prison;

(c) amend or revoke any such declaration.

(2) The prisons specified in the Schedule to these Rules are hereby declared to be prisons for the purposes of the Act and of these rules.

Code of Conduct

6.   The Secretary of State may approve a code, or codes, of conduct to have effect in relation to the conduct, duties and discipline of the staff of prisons.

Application of these rules during an emergency

7.   (1) Where there is an emergency affecting the safe and secure operation of a prison, or prisons, the Secretary of State may declare an emergency and direct that these rules shall only have effect to the extent consistent with action taken with regard to that emergency.

(2) Where any constable or other person, not being an officer, is employed by reason of any emergency to assist the governor of a prison by performing duties ordinarily performed by an officer, except in Parts XIV and XV, shall be treated as including a reference to a constable or other person so employed.

Revocation

8. The Prison Rules (Northern Ireland) 1982, The Young Offenders Centre Rules (Northern Ireland) 1982, The Prison (Amendment) Rules (Northern Ireland) 1983 and The Young Offenders Centre (Amendment) Rules (Northern Ireland) 1983 are revoked.

PART II

CLASSIFICATION, PRIVILEGES AND ACCOMMODATION

Classification

9. (1) Prisoners shall be classified in accordance with any directions made by the Secretary of State, having regard to their age, offence, length of sentence, previous record, conduct in prison or while on temporary release under rule 27 and the requirements of security, good order and discipline at the prison in which they are confined.

(2) A prisoner may be re-classified following a review by the governor taking into account any of the matters set out in paragraph (1).

(3) A prisoner shall not be re-classified as a punishment for an offence against discipline.

(4) Prisoners may be located in such part of the prison as the governor may determine by reference to their classification and any other factors which he may decide to take into account; and may subsequently be transferred to other locations in the prisons either in groups or as individuals.

(5) The classification of prisoners under this Rule will not be such as to unnecessarily deprive prisoners of the benefits of association with other persons.

Privileges

10. (1) There shall be established at every prison a system or systems of privileges appropriate to the classes of prisoners held there .

(2) The system of privileges shall have regard to prisoners' personal possessions, private cash and prison earnings in addition to access to other facilities.

(3) Where an order for the forfeiture of privileges is made by a governor under Rule 39(1) of these Rules, it shall apply only to those privileges specified in the order.

Accommodation

11. (1) Accommodation for prisoners shall be in accordance with directions approved by the Secretary of State and shall be of such size and be lighted, warmed, ventilated and fitted in such a manner as is requisite for health and human dignity subject to paragraph (4) of this Rule.

(2) Accommodation shall be provided with means by which prisoners locked inside may communicate at any time with an officer.

(3) Each prisoner shall have a separate room or cell, but where necessary the governor, in accordance with any directions approved by the Secretary of State, may accommodate two or more prisoners in a room or cell.

(4) The provision of accommodation above the standard required for the preservation of health is subject to the requirements of security and good order and to the use made of the accommodation by the prisoner or prisoners.

Cleanliness of the prison

12. (1) The governor shall take all practical steps to ensure the cleanliness and hygiene of all parts of the prison in which prisoners, officers and other staff live, work or otherwise have reason to be.

(2) To this end the governor shall consult with the medical officer and with the authorities responsible for environmental health and for health and safety at work.

(3) The governor may grant reasonable facilities to authorised officers of these authorities under paragraph (2) for the inspection of those parts of the prison in which they have a proper interest.

(4) An officer may direct a prisoner to clean and sweep the yards, passages and other parts of the prison.

Heating, lighting and ventilation

13. The governor shall ensure that the arrangements for heating, lighting and ventilation in the prison are satisfactory and the provisions of rule 12(2) and 12(3) shall apply to these matters.

Beds and bedding

14. Every prisoner shall be provided with a separate bed and with separate bedding adequate for warmth and health.

PART III

RECEPTION, TRANSFER AND DISCHARGE

General

15. No prisoner shall be received without a valid commitment order, warrant or certificate authorising his detention in custody.

Search

16. (1) Every prisoner shall be searched on reception to the prison.

(2) A prisoner may be searched before or following a visit, on any occasion on which the prisoner has come into contact with, or is likely to come into contact with, persons from outside the prison, or when his or her cell or property is searched.

(3) A search under paragraphs (1) and (2) may include a full search.

(4) The governor may direct that a prisoner or prisoners be searched at such other times as is considered necessary for the safety and security of the prison.

(5) Where the governor has grounds to believe that a prisoner is in possession of a prohibited or unauthorised article and that item may only be discovered by means of a full search the governor may direct that the prisoner be required to submit to a full search.

(6) A prisoner shall not be undressed, or required to undress, in the sight of another prisoner, or any persons other than the officers conducting the search, but a prisoner may be required to remove a hat, coat or overcoat.

(7) Any search for which a prisoner must undress may only be carried out by an officer of the same sex as the prisoner.

(8) Where a prisoner refuses to co-operate with a search, including a full search, such force as is necessary to effect the search may be used.

(9) This rule does not permit the search of a body cavity, but a prisoner may be required to open his mouth to permit a visual inspection.

(10) Under this rule a search of a prisoner may include a search of any prisoner's cell and property.

Prisoner's property on reception

17. (1) Any property or clothing which a prisoner is not allowed to retain for his own use shall be taken into safe custody under the authority and responsibility of the governor.

(2) If clothing is infested or in a state of total disrepair it may be destroyed, in which event the details shall be recorded and the prisoner informed.

(3) Any cash which a prisoner has on reception to prison shall be paid into an account under the control of the governor and the prisoner shall be credited with the amount in the books of the prison.

(4) If a prisoner has any form of medicine in his possession on reception it shall be for the medical officer to decide on its use or disposal as the case may be.

(5) If the medical officer is not on duty at the time of the reception an officer, or any other person, acting with the authority of the medical officer, will take note of any medication that a prisoner has in his possession and will take appropriate action and he will report to the medical officer before the medical officer interviews the prisoner.

Money and articles received at a prison

18. (1) Any money or other article (other than a letter or other communication) sent to a prisoner through a post office or otherwise

received at a prison shall be dealt with in accordance with the provisions of this rule and the prisoner shall be told how it is dealt with.

(2) Any cash shall, at the discretion of the governor, be-

(a) dealt with in accordance with rule 17(3); or

(b) returned to the sender if his name and address are known; or

(c) where the sender's name and address are unknown, otherwise dealt with subject to any direction by the Secretary of State provided that in relation to a prisoner committed to prison in default of payment of a sum of money, cash received at the prison shall be applied in or towards the satisfaction of the amount due from him unless the prisoner objects.

(3) Any security for money shall, at the discretion of the governor, be-

(a) placed with the prisoner's property; or

(b) returned to the sender if his name and address are known; or

(c) encashed and the cash dealt with in accordance with paragraph (2) of this rule.

(4) Any other article to which this rule applies shall, at the discretion of the governor, be-

(a) delivered to the prisoner or placed with his property; or

(b) returned to the sender if his name or address are known; or

(c) if the sender's name and address are not known or if the article is of such a nature that it would be unreasonable to return it, sold or otherwise disposed of, and the net proceeds of any sale dealt with in accordance with paragraph (2) of this rule.

Record, photograph and finger-prints

19. (1) The name, age, height, weight, distinctive marks and any measurements or other particulars which may be required in regard to a prisoner shall, on his reception and subsequently as necessary, be taken and recorded in such a way as the Secretary of State may direct.

(2) A convicted prisoner may be photographed, palm-printed and finger-printed on reception and at subsequent times as may be necessary for the purposes of prison records.

(3) No copy of a photograph of a prisoner, or other personal details taken in under this rule, may be given to any person not authorised to receive them.

Baths

20. Every prisoner on his reception shall have a hot bath or shower as directed by the governor or medical officer unless exempted by either from doing so.

Medical exemption on reception

21. (1) Subject to paragraph (2) the medical officer or other approved medical practitioner shall separately examine every prisoner as early as practicable on the day of his reception and shall record the result.

(2) If a prisoner is received too late on the day of his reception, or if he is received on a day when the medical officer is not on duty at the prison, he shall be seen following his reception by an officer, or any other person, acting with the authority of the medical officer, and then be examined by the medical officer as soon as possible on the next day or where that is not possible within 48 hours of his reception.

(3) The medical officer shall not authorise anyone to see a prisoner under paragraph (2) unless he is satisfied that they are adequately trained.

(4) If any prisoner is found to have any infectious disease or to be in any condition which may threaten the health or well-being of

others, the medical officer shall report the matter to the governor and the chief medical officer and steps shall at once be taken to treat the disease or condition appropriately.

Interview with governor after reception

22. The governor shall interview every prisoner as soon as practicable after his reception, and shall ensure that any relevant matters to which the prisoner may draw attention are noted and dealt with.

Information to prisoners

23. (1) As soon as practicable after reception every prisoner shall be provided with information sufficient to enable him to understand the disciplinary and other requirements of the prison, the facilities available and the proper methods of seeking further information and of making complaints.

(2) Information provided under this rule shall be made available in writing for a prisoner to consult in his own time.

(3) In the case of a prisoner who cannot read or who for any reason has difficulty in understanding, the governor shall ensure that the necessary information has been properly explained to him.

(4) A prisoner may consult these rules at any reasonable time and a prisoner shall be informed during reception of the right to do so.

Foreign nationals

24. (1) Foreign nationals shall be informed without delay that they may communicate with the appropriate diplomatic representative of the state to which they belong and be given reasonable facilities to do so.

(2) Refugees or stateless persons shall be given reasonable facilities to communicate with the diplomatic representative of the state which looks after their interests, or any national or international authority which serves the interests of such persons.

(3) Special arrangements shall be made to meet the needs of foreign nationals with linguistic difficulties.

Custody outside prison

25. (1) Subject to paragraph (2) and (5) a prisoner who is directed by any court or by the Secretary of State to be taken to any place shall be kept in the custody of the officers ordered by the governor to take him to that place.

(2) A prisoner who is directed to be brought before a court of summary jurisdiction may be kept in the custody of police officers outside a prison.

(3) When a prisoner is being transferred to or from prison, he shall be exposed to public view as little as possible, and as far as is practicable be protected from insult, curiosity and publicity of any kind.

(4) Prisoners shall on all occasions be transported in conditions which avoid any unnecessary physical hardship or indignity.

(5) A prisoner having been removed from prison and detained in hospital shall remain under the control of the governor of that prison and may be kept in the custody of an officer, a police officer or any person to whose custody he may be temporarily be committed with the approval of the governor.

Transfer

26. (1) Where practicable, every prisoner shall be interviewed by the governor before transfer.

(2) The medical officer shall see every prisoner as short a time as is practicable before his transfer to another prison unless, in exceptional circumstances and for reasons of security or the good order and control of the prison, the governor directs that the transfer must take effect immediately.

(3) If the medical officer is of the opinion that the prisoner is not fit to be transferred he shall inform the governor of that and the prisoner shall not be transferred.

(4) Where a prisoner is transferred from one prison to another he shall be allowed reasonable facilities to inform his next-of-kin and if he is an unconvicted prisoner or engaged in litigation, his legal advisor.

Temporary release

27. (1) A prisoner to whom this rule applies may be temporarily released for any period or periods and subject to any conditions.

(2) A prisoner may be temporarily released under this rule for any special purpose or to enable him to have medical treatment , to engage in employment, to receive instruction or training or to assist him in his transition from prison to outside life.

(3) A prisoner released under this rule may be recalled to prison at any time whether the conditions of his release have been broken or not.

(4) This rule applies to prisoners other than persons-

(a) remanded in custody by any court; or

(b) committed in custody for trial; or

(c) committed to be sentenced or otherwise dealt with before or by the Crown Court.

Discharge

28. (1) Every prisoner shall be interviewed by the governor before discharge.

(2) The medical officer shall examine every prisoner as short a time as is practicable before his discharge.

(3) On the discharge of a prisoner his own clothes and other property shall, subject to paragraph (4), be returned to him.

(4) If a prisoner's clothes have been destroyed under rule 17(2) suitable clothing shall be provided for him.

Death or serious illness of prisoner

29. (1) If a prisoner dies, becomes seriously ill, sustains any serious injury or is removed to hospital, the governor shall, if he knows the address, at once inform the prisoner's next-of-kin, and also any person the prisoner may reasonably have asked should be informed.

(2) If a prisoner dies, the governor shall immediately notify the coroner having jurisdiction, the board of visitors and the Secretary of State.

(3) If a prisoner dies, the medical officer shall record and report to the governor and the chief medical officer-

(a) when the deceased was injured or taken ill;

(b) the time at which he was first told of the injury or illness;

(c) the nature of the injury or disease;

(d) when the prisoner died;

and in cases where a post-mortem examination is made, the medical officer shall report on its findings and make any observations which he considers appropriate.

Remission of sentence

30. (1) A prisoner serving a sentence of imprisonment for an actual term of more than five days may, on the ground of his good conduct, be granted remission in accordance with the provisions of this rule, but this rule shall not permit the reduction of the actual term to less than five days.

(2) The remission granted shall not exceed half the total of the actual term and any period spent in custody which is taken into account under section 26(2) of the Treatment of Offenders Act (Northern Ireland) 1968 (which relates to the duration of sentences).

(3) Where a prisoner commits an offence while in prison custody or on temporary release under rule 27 and is awarded a sentence to be served concurrently with the sentence that was being served when the offence was committed the governor may order that the prisoner shall lose remission in respect of all or part of that sentence up to a maximum of 28 days or with the authority of the Secretary of State for up to 180 days.

(4) Remission lost under paragraph (3) may be restored by the governor, or if it is more than 28 days, the Secretary of State.

(5) The foregoing provisions of this rule shall have effect subject to any disciplinary award of loss of remission and shall not apply to a sentence of imprisonment for life.

(6) A prisoner who would otherwise be discharged on any of the following days, that is to say-

(a) a Sunday, Christmas Day, Good Friday;

(b) a public holiday in Northern Ireland;

(c) in the case of a person who is serving a term (as pronounced) of more than seven days, a Saturday;

(d) a day on which he would be granted temporary release under rule 27; may be discharged on the next preceding day which is not one of these days.

(7) In this rule "actual term" means the term of a sentence of imprisonment as reduced by section 26(2) of the Treatment of Offenders Act (Northern Ireland) 1968 and, in the case of a sentence pronounced outside Northern Ireland, any reference to the said section 26(2) includes a reference to any corresponding provision having effect where the sentence was pronounced.

(8) For the purposes of this rule -

(a) consecutive terms of imprisonment and, in the case of terms of imprisonment imposed before 1st March 1976, terms which are wholly or partly concurrent shall be treated as a single term;

(b) a person committed to prison in default of a payment of a sum adjudged to be paid by a conviction shall be treated as serving a sentence of imprisonment;

(c) a person ordered to be returned to prison under article 3 of the Treatment of Offenders Act (Northern Ireland) 1976 shall be treated as serving a sentence of imprisonment.

(9) Paragraphs (1) and (2) of this rule have effect subject to sections 14 and 15 of the Northern Ireland (Emergency Provisions) Act 1991 which restrict the remission available to prisoners convicted of scheduled offences.

PART IV

DISCIPLINE AND CONTROL

Supervision

31. (1) Prisoners may be supervised by officers of either sex.

(2) In circumstances in which privacy would be expected a prisoner will be supervised by an officer of the same sex.

Restriction of association

32. (1) Where it is necessary for the maintenance of good order or discipline, or in his own interests that the association permitted to a prisoner should be restricted, either generally or for particular purposes, the governor may arrange for the restriction of his association.

(2) A prisoner's association under this rule may not be restricted under this rule for a period of more than 48 hours without the agreement of a member of the board of visitors or the Secretary of State.

(3) An extension of the period of restriction under paragraph (2) shall be for a period not exceeding one month, but may be renewed for further periods, each not exceeding one month.

(4) The governor may arrange at his discretion for such a prisoner as aforesaid to resume full or increased association with other prisoners and shall do so if in any case the medical officer so advises on medical grounds.

(5) Rule 55(1) shall not apply to a prisoner who is subject to restriction of association under this rule but such a prisoner shall be entitled to one hour of exercise each day which shall be taken in the open air, weather permitting.

Unauthorised articles

33. A governor may confiscate any article which a prisoner is not allowed to have in his possession after his reception into prison.

Prohibited articles

34. (1) Except as provided by statute, or with the authority of the Secretary of State in the case of firearms, or the governor in regard to all other items, no person may-

(a) bring, send, throw or cause to be taken into a prison by post or otherwise; or

(b) bring, take or throw out of a prison; or

(c) deposit in any place with intent that it should come into a prisoner's possession

any weapon, money, clothing, food, drink, drug, tobacco, letter, parcel, package, paper, book, implement or other article.

(2) Any item introduced contrary to paragraph (1) may be confiscated by the governor and shall then be dealt with as the Secretary of State may direct.

Laying of disciplinary charges

35. (1) Where a prisoner is to be charged with an offence against prison discipline the charge shall be laid in writing before the governor within 48 hours of the discovery of the offence save in exceptional circumstances.

(2) The prisoner shall be informed of the charge and the grounds on which it has been made within 24 hours of the charge being laid before the governor and, in any case, before the inquiry by the governor, to enable him to consider any defence he may wish to make.

(3) Before any inquiry the prisoner who has been charged will be provided with information about the procedure and purpose of the inquiry and will be informed of the right to request legal representation at the inquiry.

(4) A prisoner who is to be charged with an offence against discipline may be kept apart from other prisoners pending adjudication, if the governor considers that it is necessary, but may not be held separately for more than 48 hours.

Inquiry into charge

36. (1) The governor shall hold an inquiry into any charge that a prisoner has committed an offence against prison discipline.

(2) The governor shall first inquire into any charge not later, save in exceptional circumstances, than the next day after the laying of the charge unless that day is a Saturday, Sunday or public holiday, or is a day of religious observance for the prisoner in accordance with his religious denomination as recorded under rule 57.

(3) The governor may adjourn the inquiry pending further investigations, but must give reasons for doing so which shall be recorded in the record made under rule 37; any adjournment must not unfairly prejudice the interests of the prisoner.

(4) At any inquiry into a charge against a prisoner the governor shall satisfy himself that the prisoner has had sufficient time to prepare his defence; the prisoner shall be given a full opportunity of hearing what is alleged against him and of presenting his own case.

(5) If the governor is not satisfied that the prisoner has had sufficient time to prepare his case he may allow an adjournment sufficient to allow the prisoner to prepare his case.

(6) Every charge against a prisoner shall be dealt with by the governor or, in a prison where a deputy governor has been appointed, by the deputy governor; but where neither the governor nor the deputy governor is available the governor may delegate the inquiry to another governor authorised by the Secretary of State to deal with charges.

(7) A reference to the governor in paragraph (1) and rules 37, 39 and 40 shall include a reference to a deputy or other officer authorised to deal with the charge under paragraph (6).

Findings

37. (1) A record will be kept of every inquiry into an offence against prison discipline and shall include the charge preferred, the facts alleged, a summary of the evidence presented, the governor's findings and, if the charge is upheld, any award made against the prisoner.

(2) The governor may find a prisoner guilty of a lesser charge if it appears to him appropriate to do so and if it would not unfairly prejudice the interests of the prisoner. If the governor does so he shall give his reasons in the record made under paragraph (1).

Offences against prison discipline

38. A prisoner shall be guilty of an offence against prison discipline, if he or she -

(1) mutinies or commits any act of collective indiscipline;

(2) assaults an officer or other member of staff;

(3) commits an assault causing injury against any other person including another prisoner;

(4) commits any other assault;

(5) fights or wrestles with any prisoner or other person;

(6) escapes or absconds from prison or legal custody;

(7) endangers the health or personal safety of any person or persons, including prisoners, through intentional or reckless conduct;

(8) detains any person against his will;

(9) intentionally obstructs an officer in the execution of his duty or any other person going about his authorised duties within the prison;

(10) denies access to any part of a prison to any officer or other authorised person;

(11) fails to comply with a condition of temporary release under rule 27;

(12) has in his possession any unauthorised article, or a greater quantity of any article that he is authorised to have, or sells or delivers to or receives from any person any unauthorised article, or sells, or without permission, delivers to any person any article which he is allowed to have only for his own use;

(13) takes improperly any article belonging to another person or to a prison;

(14) intentionally or recklessly sets fire to any part of a prison or any property, whether or not his own, or, destroys or damages any part of a prison or other property not being his own;

(15) absents himself from any place where he is required to be or is present at any place where he is not authorised to be;

(16) is disrespectful to any person or uses threatening, abusive or insulting words or behaviour;

(17) pierces himself or another prisoner with a needle or other implement, or consents to another prisoner piercing him with a needle or other implement, for the purpose of making a tattoo, for bodily piercing (including ear piercing), or for any other purpose.

(18) commits an indecent or obscene act;

(19) prepares, manufactures, consumes inhales or administers to himself or any other prisoner, with or without consent, any intoxicating substance or drug, or buys, sells or passes or possesses any such item.

(20) bribes or attempts to influence any officer or other person going about authorised duties within a prison;

(21) being required to work refuses to do so, or intentionally fails to work properly;

(22) disobeys any lawful order;

(23) disobeys or fails to comply with any rule or regulation applying to him;

(24) in any other way offends against good order and discipline;

(25) attempts to commit, incites another prisoner to commit, or assists another prisoner to commit or attempt to commit any of the foregoing offences.

Governor's awards

39. (1) The governor may, subject to rules 40 and 41 make one or more of the following awards for an offence against prison discipline-

(a) caution;

(b) loss of remission for a period not exceeding 28 days;

(c) stoppage of earnings for a period not exceeding 28 days;

(d) stoppage of any or all privileges other than earnings, for a period not exceeding 28 days or 90 days in the case of evening association;

(e) exclusion from associated work for a period not exceeding 14 days;

(f) cellular confinement for a period not exceeding 3 days.

(2) A prisoner found guilty of an offence against discipline under rule 38(14) may, in addition to or in lieu of an award of stoppage of earnings under paragraph (1)(c), be required to pay a sum out of earnings thereafter made by him.

(3) Such a sum shall not exceed one half of the prisoner's earnings for the week in which the offence was committed, and the rate of reduction from earnings shall not exceed one half of the prisoner's earnings in any one week.

(4) If a prisoner is found guilty of more than one charge arising out of an incident, punishments under this rule may be ordered to run consecutively, but in the case of forfeiture of remission of sentence the total period forfeited shall not exceed 28 days and in the case of cellular confinement the total period shall not exceed 14 days.

More serious offences - inquiry and awards by the Secretary of State or board of visitors

40. (1) Where a prisoner is charged with an offence under rule 38 paragraph 9 (1), (2), (3), (6) or (8) or any other offence under rule 38 for which in the view of the governor it may be appropriate to award a more serious punishment than is provided for in rule 39, the governor, unless he dismisses the charge, may refer the charge to the Secretary of State.

(2) The Secretary of State shall thereupon inquire into the charge and, if he is satisfied that the offence has been committed, may make one or more of the following awards-

(a) caution;

(b) loss of remission for a period not exceeding 90 days;

(c) stoppage of earnings for a period not exceeding 56 days;

(d) stoppage of all or any privileges other than earnings, for a period not exceeding 90 days or 180 days in the case of evening association;

(e) exclusion from associated work for a period not exceeding 14 days;

(f) cellular confinement for a period not exceeding 56 days.

(3) Where a prisoner is found guilty of an offence under rule 38(14) the provisions of rule 39(2) and (3) will apply.

(4) The Secretary of State may delegate his powers under this rule to the board of visitors or to a panel appointed from all the boards of visitors for the purpose of hearing charges in any particular case.

Provisions in relation to particular awards

41. (1) In the case of an offence against prison discipline committed by a prisoner who is detained only on remand or to await trial or sentence,

an award of loss of remission may be made as provided in rules 39 and 40 notwithstanding that the prisoner has not (or had not at the time of the offence) been sentenced to imprisonment or ordered to be detained in a young offenders centre.

(2) An award under paragraph (1) shall have effect only where the sentence of imprisonment or term of detention in a young offenders centre being imposed is reduced by section 26(2) of the Treatment of Offenders Act (Northern Ireland) 1968 by a period which includes the time when the offence against discipline was committed.

(3) As regards a person detained in a young offenders centre, no award under this rule shall have effect to the extent, if any, that the award made was more severe than could, at the time it was made, have been made under the rules applying to the centre.

Suspended awards

43. (1) Subject to any directions by the Secretary of State, the power to make a disciplinary award (other than a caution) shall include the power to direct that the award is not to take effect unless, during a period specified in the direction (not being more than six months from the date of the direction), the prisoner commits another offence against discipline and a direction is given under paragraph (2).

(2) Where a prisoner commits an offence against prison discipline during the period specified in a direction given under paragraph (1) the authority dealing with that offence may-

(a) direct that the suspended award shall take effect; or

(b) reduce the period or amount of the suspended award and direct that it shall take effect as so reduced; or

(c) vary the original direction by substituting for the period specified therein a period expiring not later than 6 months from the period of the variation; or

(d) give no direction in respect of the suspended award.

Remission and mitigation of awards

44. (1) The Secretary of State may quash any finding of guilt or remit any punishment or mitigate it.

(2) Subject to any directions of the Secretary of State the governor may remit or mitigate any punishment imposed by a governor and

the board of visitors may remit or mitigate any punishment imposed by a board of visitors.

(3) In this rule mitigate means reducing the punishment or substituting another punishment which is, in the opinion of the Secretary of State, the governor or, as the case may be, the board of visitors, less severe.

Petition against awards

45. (1) A prisoner may petition the Secretary of State in respect of an award made by a governor or by the board of visitors.

(2) A petition will only be permitted under this section where it alleges that-

(a) the facts established did not justify a finding of guilt;

(b) the governor or board of visitors misapplied the prison rules or failed to follow the principles of natural justice;

(c) the award was more severe than was merited by the findings; or

(d) any combination of the above.

(3) The petition will be considered on its merits and a response in writing sent to the prisoner as soon as possible.

(4) Where a petition is upheld any of the remedies provided for under rule 44(1) may be applied as appropriate.

Use of force

46. (1) Any officer in dealing with a prisoner shall not use force unnecessarily.

(2) If force is necessary no more force should be used than is necessary in the circumstances prevailing.

(3) If force is used, for whatever reason, the officer or officers concerned shall report details to the governor as soon as possible.

Temporary confinement

47. (1) For the purpose of preventing disturbance, damage or injury, a refractory or violent prisoner may be temporarily confined in a special room or protected room approved for the purpose by the Secretary of State; but a prisoner shall not be confined in such a cell as a punishment or after he has ceased to be refractory or violent.

(2) The governor shall inform the medical officer of the intended removal of any prisoner to a special cell or protected room, but where this is not possible the medical officer shall be informed as soon as possible thereafter.

(3) Notwithstanding the provisions of paragraphs (1) and (2) the medical officer may, for the purpose of preventing a prisoner from causing injury to himself or to others, order that he may be temporarily confined in a protected room and to be confined there for as long as the medical officer considers necessary.

(4) The governor, the Secretary of State and a member of the board of visitors shall be informed of any prisoner who is so confined.

(5) Every prisoner who is temporarily confined in a special cell or protected room shall be visited at least once a day by the governor and by the medical officer.

(6) Every prisoner so confined shall be observed at least once every 15 minutes by an officer and a record shall be kept of such observations.

Restraints

48. (1) Where it is necessary to prevent a prisoner from injuring himself or others, damaging property or creating a disturbance, the governor may order him to be put under restraint.

(2) Notice of such an order shall be given without delay to a member of the board of visitors, the medical officer and to the Secretary of State.

(3) On receipt of the notice the medical officer shall inform the governor whether he concurs with the order and the governor shall give effect to any recommendation that the medical officer may make.

(4) Except as provided by this rule no prisoner shall be put under restraint otherwise than for their safe custody during transfer or on medical grounds by order of the medical officer.

(5) No prisoner shall be put under restraint as a punishment.

(6) No prisoner shall be kept under restraint longer than is necessary.

(7) A governor may only order that a prisoner be kept under restraint for more than 24 hours with the agreement of both the medical officer and a member of the board of visitors.

(8) Where an authorisation is given under paragraph (7) it shall be reviewed daily by the governor and the medical officer.

(9) Every prisoner who is under restraint shall be observed at intervals of not more than 15 minutes by an officer and a record shall be kept of such observations.

(10) The governor shall record the particulars of every case of restraint.

(11) Any means of restraint shall be of a pattern authorised by the Secretary of State and shall be used in such manner and under such conditions as he may direct.

General control of admission to the prison

49. (1) No person may enter the prison without the governor's permission, unless he is entitled to do so.

(2) Any person entering or leaving the prison may be stopped, examined and, with their consent, searched.

(3) Such person shall be searched only by officers of the same sex as that person.

(4) Any person who does not consent to being searched may be denied access to the prison.

(5) The governor may direct the removal from the prison of any person who does not leave on being required to do so.

(6) Under this rule a search of person may include a search of any item in that person's possession or of a vehicle.

Visitors viewing the prison

50. (1) No outside person shall be permitted to view a prison unless authorised to do so by statute or by the Secretary of State.

(2) No person viewing the prison shall be authorised to make a sketch, or take a photograph or make a film or sound recording or communicate with a prisoner unless authorised to do so by statute or by the Secretary of State.

(3) In paragraph (2) "film" includes any record however made of a sequence of visual images which is capable of being used as a means of showing that sequence as a moving picture.

PART V

WORK, EDUCATION AND RECREATION

Work

51. (1) Work of a useful nature or other purposeful activities shall be provided to keep prisoners actively employed during their normal day.

(2) Any prisoner may be required to work by the governor unless excused by the medical officer on medical grounds.

(3) No prisoner shall be employed on any class of work unless the medical officer has certified him as fit for that class of work.

(4) No prisoner may be required to work for more than 8 hours in any day and any prisoner engaged in a regular pattern of work shall have at least one day rest a week.

(5) As far as practicable, work shall be provided outside the cells and in association with other prisoners.

(6) No prisoner shall be employed except on work of an appropriate nature authorised by the Secretary of State.

(7) Except with the authority of the Secretary of State, no prisoner shall be employed in the service of any other prisoner or of any other officer or for the private benefit of any person.

(8) Prisoners who are recorded as members of a religious denomination under rule 57 shall not be required to work unnecessarily on their days of religious observance.

(9) For the purpose of these rules "work" includes employment in the ordinary service of the prison, in prison occupational services and participation in vocational training.

(10) The Secretary of State may make arrangements for prisoners to earn money for work carried out under this rule.

Education

52. (1) Every prisoner who expresses interest in participating in education shall be permitted to do so to the extent practicable; special attention shall be paid to prisoners with problems of illiteracy or innumeracy.

(2) Programmes of educational classes covering as wide a range of subjects as practicable shall be arranged at every prison.

(3) As far as practicable, reasonable facilities shall also be made available to prisoners who wish to improve their education by correspondence courses or private study.

(4) Where a prisoner is engaged in education during a period in which he could otherwise have worked he shall be allowed earnings in accordance with rule 51(10) of these rules.

(5) As soon as possible after his reception or following his transfer to another prison, every prisoner shall be informed of the educational facilities which are available.

(6) Where a prisoner's educational activities are interrupted by his transfer to another prison or for any other reason, every effort shall be made to assist him to continue with them.

Handicrafts and hobbies

53. As far as practicable reasonable facilities shall be allowed to prisoners who wish to practice handicrafts or other hobbies.

Libraries

54. (1) A library shall be provided in every prison and every prisoner shall be allowed to have books or other items borrowed from the library, and to exchange them, under such conditions as the governor or the Secretary of State may determine.

(2) As far as practicable, and subject to the requirements of security, control and good order, prisoners shall be allowed to go to the library and to choose their books or other items there.

Exercise and association

55. (1) Every prisoner shall be given the opportunity of association for not less than one hour each day which may be taken as exercise in the open air, weather permitting.

(2) Where on any day a prisoner participates in exercise consisting of sport or physical training indoors, or is engaged in outside work the requirement that association be taken as exercise in paragraph (1) shall not apply.

(3) The medical officer shall decide upon the fitness of every prisoner for exercise, sport and physical training and may excuse a prisoner from, or modify, any such activity on medical grounds.

(5) Where necessary, special arrangements shall be made, in consultation with the medical officer, for remedial physical education or therapy.

PART VI

RELIGION

General

56. All prisoners shall be allowed to practise their religion to the extent compatible with good order and discipline.

Religious denomination

57. (1) On reception each prisoner shall be required to state his religious denomination, if any, and the governor shall record the denomination so stated.

(2) A prisoner may change his recorded religious denomination with the agreement of the governor.

Chaplains

58. (1) A chaplain in carrying out his duties shall support the governor.

(2) A chaplain may be subject to the rules and regulations of the prison.

Duties of chaplains

59. (1) A chaplain shall interview individually every prisoner who is recorded as belonging to his denomination and is willing to be interviewed-

> (a) as soon as possible after his reception;

> (b) from time to time as often as practicable during his imprisonment; and

> (c) a short time before his discharge.

(2) A chaplain shall give such religious instruction as may be practicable to any prisoner of his denomination wishing it.

(3) A chaplain shall conduct divine service for prisoners of his denomination at such times as may be arranged.

(4) A chaplain shall, as often as possible, visit all prisoners of his denomination who are sick, under restraint, or confined to a cell.

(5) A chaplain shall, if no other arrangements are made, read the burial service at the funeral of any prisoner of his denomination who dies in the prison.

(6) The Secretary of State may require a chaplain to report to him on the carrying out of any of his duties as a chaplain.

Substitute for chaplain

60. (1) A person or persons, not exceeding 3 in number, approved by the Secretary of State, may act for the chaplain in his absence, and any such person or persons shall be subject to the rules and regulations of the prison in like manner as a chaplain.

(2) Any person or persons approved by the Secretary of State may assist the chaplain in the carrying out of religious services or in such other duties as may be approved.

(3) The Secretary of State may withdraw any such approval so granted.

Visits by chaplains of other denominations

61. (1) As far as practicable access to a chaplain of any religious denomination shall not be refused to any prisoner.

(2) Any request by a prisoner to see a chaplain of a denomination other than that of his recorded denomination shall be passed to the chaplain concerned and unless the prisoner requests otherwise, the chaplain of the prisoner's denomination shall also be informed.

(3) If a prisoner objects to the visit of any religious representative, he shall not be compelled to receive the visit.

Visits by other ministers

62. (1) Where a prisoner belongs to a denomination for which no chaplain has been appointed the governor shall do what he reasonably can, if so requested by the prisoner, to arrange for him to be visited regularly by a minister of that denomination.

(2) Without prejudice to paragraph (1), any other request by a prisoner to see a minister of any denomination may be permitted at the governor's discretion and unless the prisoner requests otherwise, the chaplain of the prisoner's denomination shall be informed.

(3) Any minister as referred to in paragraphs (1) and (2) shall be subject to the rules and regulations that apply to visitors to a prison.

Privacy

63. Any interview under this part shall be accorded a degree of privacy appropriate to its nature and purpose.

Religious books

64. (1) Every prisoner shall be allowed to have a Bible or other appropriate religious written material approved by his denomination.

(2) There shall, as far as reasonably practicable, be available for every prisoner's personal use such other religious books as his denomination recognises.

(3) So far as is practicable, every prisoner shall be allowed to satisfy the needs of his religious, spiritual and moral life by having in his possession any other necessary or other appropriate material not provided under paragraphs (1) and (2).

PART VI

SOCIAL RELATIONS AND COMMUNICATIONS

Family relationships, welfare and other care

65. (1) Special attention shall be paid to the maintenance of relationships between a prisoner and his family.

(2) Prisoners shall be encouraged and assisted to establish and maintain such relations with persons and agencies outside prison as may, in the opinion of the governor, best promote the interests of the family and his own social rehabilitation.

(3) From the beginning of a prisoner's sentence, consideration shall be given, in consultation with all appropriate persons and agencies, to the prisoner's future and any practical assistance which he can be given on and after his release.

(4) The governor shall ensure that any officer with responsibility for prisoner's welfare is provided with appropriate facilities to carry out his duties.

Current affairs

66. (1) Prisoners shall be allowed to keep themselves informed of current affairs by such means as may be permitted by the governor.

(2) A prisoner may receive newspapers and periodicals subject to any restrictions imposed by the governor.

Communications

67. (1) The Secretary of State may, with a view to securing discipline and good order or the prevention of crime or in the interests of any persons, impose restrictions, either generally or in a particular case, on the communications to be permitted between a prisoner and other persons.

(2) The governor may at any time, having regard to circumstances obtaining or expected to obtain in the prison, suspend all or any visits for such period as the Secretary of State may approve.

(3) Except as provided by statute or in these rules, a prisoner shall not be permitted to communicate with any outside person, or that person with him, without the authority of the Secretary of State.

(4) Except as provided in these rules, every letter or communication to or from a prisoner may be read or examined by the governor who may, at his discretion, stop any such letter or communication on the grounds that it is not permitted under paragraph (1) or that it may undermine the security of the prison.

(5) Every visit to a prisoner shall take place within the sight of an officer, unless the Secretary of State otherwise directs.

(6) Except as provided by these rules, every visit to a prisoner shall take place within the hearing of an officer, unless the Secretary of State otherwise directs.

(7) The Secretary of State may give directions, generally or in relation to any visit or class of visits, concerning the days and times when a prisoner may be visited and the duration of such visits.

(8) Visits shall not take place on a Sunday except with the permission of the Secretary of State.

(9) Except with the governor's authority, not more than three persons shall be allowed to visit a prisoner at one time.

Personal letters and visits

68. (1) A prisoner shall be entitled to send and receive a letter on his reception to prison.

(2) A prisoner is entitled to send and receive one letter each week, but the Secretary of State may, as a privilege allow additional letters to be sent and received by any class of prisoners.

(3) A prisoner is entitled to a visit once in a period of 4 weeks, but the Secretary of State may as a privilege allow additional visits to any class of prisoner.

(4) The governor may allow additional letters or visits in any particular case.

(5) The governor may allow a prisoner entitled to a visit to send and receive a letter instead.

(6) The governor may defer the right of a prisoner to a visit until the expiration of any period of cellular confinement.

(7) Save in exceptional circumstances, visits under this rule shall be of at least 30 minutes duration.

(8) A prisoner shall not be entitled under this rule to receive a visit from any person other than a relative or friend, except with the leave of the governor or the Secretary of State.

(9) Any letter or visit under the succeeding provisions of these rules shall not be counted as a letter or visit for the purposes of this rule.

Police interviews

69. (1) A police officer may, on production of an order issued by or on behalf of the Chief Constable of the Royal Ulster Constabulary, interview any prisoner.

(2) An interview under this rule shall take place in the sight of, and if the governor directs, within the hearing of a prison officer.

Securing release

70. (1) A person detained in prison in default of finding a surety, or of payment of a sum of money, may communicate with, and be visited at any reasonable time on a weekday by any relative or friend to arrange for a surety or payment in order to secure his release from prison.

(2) Every prisoner detained as specified in paragraph (1) shall be told of this rule on his reception.

71. (1) Reasonable facilities shall be allowed for the legal adviser of a prisoner who is party to legal proceedings, civil or criminal, to interview the prisoner in connection with those proceedings in the sight but not in the hearing of an officer.

(2) A prisoner's legal adviser may, with the Secretary of State's permission, interview the prisoner in connection with any other legal business in the sight but not in the hearing of an officer.

Correspondence in connection with legal matters

72. (1) A prisoner who is party to any legal proceedings may correspond with his legal adviser or any court, national or international, in connection with those proceedings.

(2) A prisoner may correspond with a solicitor for the purpose of obtaining legal advice concerning any matter in relation to which he may become a party to legal proceedings or for the purpose of instructing the solicitor to issue proceedings, or to allow him to conduct any legal business.

(3) A prisoner shall on request be provided with any writing materials necessary for the purpose of paragraph (1).

(4) No letter to which this rule applies shall be opened by the governor unless he has reason to believe that it contains matter not related to actual or potential legal proceedings or other legal business.

(5) Subject to any directions given in the particular case by the Secretary of State, a registered medical practitioner selected by or on

behalf of a prisoner to whom paragraph (1) applies shall be afforded reasonable facilities for examining him in connection with the proceedings and may do so out of hearing but in the sight of an officer.

Control of visitors to prisoners

73. (1) The governor may require the name and address of any visitor to a prisoner and may require the visitor to be searched.

(2) Any search under this rule requires the consent of the visitor and if the visitor does not consent the governor may refuse the visitor admission.

(3) Where the governor denies admission to any visitor he shall record his reasons for doing so.

(4) No search of a visitor shall be made in the presence of any prisoner or other visitor or by, or in the presence of, an officer of the other sex.

(5) If there are reasonable grounds for suspecting that anyone visiting a prisoner is bringing in or taking out any article for an improper purpose, or contrary to the rules and regulations of the prison, or that his conduct may tend to subvert discipline or good order, the governor may suspend his visit and remove him from the prison.

(6) Where a visit is suspended under paragraph (3) the fact shall be recorded and reported to the Secretary of State.

(7) A copy of the law regarding the introduction of prohibited articles into the prison shall be displayed in the visiting area and, before the prisoner is brought into that area, the visitor's attention shall be drawn to it.

PART VIII

PRISONERS' REQUESTS AND COMPLAINTS

General

74. (1) A prisoner may make any request or complaint relating to his imprisonment to an officer, a governor, a member of the board of visitors or an officer of the Secretary of State visiting the prison.

(2) Any such request or complaint shall be recorded by the person to whom it is made and shall be reported as soon as possible to the governor.

(3) A prisoner may make a request or complaint orally or in writing.

(4) Every request and complaint shall be considered, and a reply given, as soon as possible.

(5) If a prisoner wishes to make a request or complaint relating to an incident or event, he should do so at an appropriate time.

Requests to see the governor

75. On every day other than at weekends or public holidays the governor shall hear any request made to him under rule 74 above.

Requests to see a member of the board of visitors

76. On the occasion of each visit to the prison by a member of the board of visitors, the governor shall inform him of all outstanding requests by prisoners to see a member of the board.

Requests to see an officer of the Secretary of State

77. On the occasion of each visit to the prison by an officer of the Secretary of State the governor shall inform such an officer of all outstanding requests by prisoners to see him.

78. (1) A prisoner may make a written complaint in confidence to the governing governor or to the chairman of the board of visitors; such complaints shall be delivered to the recipient as soon as possible.

(2) A prisoner who makes a complaint under this rule shall be informed that if his complaint involves any prison officer or other

staff, it may be necessary to make the complaint known to those persons so that it can be fully investigated.

Petitions to the Secretary of State

79. (1) A prisoner may petition the Secretary of State about any matter relating to his imprisonment.

(2) Petitions to the Secretary of State shall be despatched by the governor as soon as possible with any relevant information to assist the Secretary of State in considering the petition.

(3) A prisoner may make a petition to the Secretary of State in a sealed envelope.

(4) A petition sent under paragraph (3) shall be forwarded unopened unless the governor has reason to believe that other material is enclosed; the petition itself shall not be read at the prison before it is forwarded.

(5) A prisoner who intends to send a petition under paragraph (3) shall be informed that if it involves the governor, any prison officer or other member of staff, it is likely to be necessary to make the contents known to those persons so that it can be investigated.

(6) The Secretary of State may pass a petition received under this rule to a governor of a prison if it relates to a matter under his authority and in such a case the governor will investigate and reply to the petition.

PART IX

PHYSICAL WELFARE

Medical provision

80. At every prison a separate building or a suitable part of the prison shall be equipped, furnished and staffed in a way appropriate to the medical care and treatment of sick prisoners.

Hygiene

81. (1) Every prisoner shall be allowed adequate access to sanitation facilities and water for health and cleanliness and will be provided with an appropriate range of toilet articles, which shall be replaced as necessary.

(2) Every prisoner shall be required to keep himself clean by washing at proper times and by having a hot bath or shower at least once a week unless excused by the governor or medical officer.

(3) Every male prisoner may be required to shave as necessary for health and cleanliness.

(4) A prisoner's hair shall not be cut without his consent unless the medical officer considers it necessary for the sake of health and cleanliness.

(5) A governor may require that a prisoner cover or restrain his hair at such times as are necessary for the protection of health and hygiene.

(6) Every prisoner shall keep his cell, utensils, books and other articles issued for his use, and his clothing and bedding, clean and neatly arranged.

Food

82. (1) Every prisoner shall be provided with sufficient food which is wholesome, nutritious, palatable and adequately presented and well prepared and which takes into account age, health and work and, as far as practicable, religious or cultural requirements.

(2) Unless the governor or the medical officer directs, no prisoner shall be allowed to have any food other than that normally provided.

(3) A prisoner who wishes to complain about the food supplied to him must make the complaint as soon as possible after he has received the food; any such complaint shall be properly considered by the governor and, where appropriate, action to remedy the complaint shall be taken as soon as possible.

(4) The governor shall ensure that the condition, quality and quantity of food, both before and after it is cooked and at the point of delivery, and the conditions under which it is prepared, are inspected frequently and that appropriate action is taken as soon as possible where any shortcoming is discovered.

(5) The medical officer shall satisfy himself that the nature, quality and quantity of food is appropriate to prisoners' health.

(6) A member of the board of visitors shall, on behalf of the board, inspect the preparation and delivery of prisoners' food and its palatability at frequent intervals.

(7) In this rule "food" includes drink.

Alcohol, drugs and tobacco

83. (1) A prisoner shall not be given or allowed to have any intoxicating liquor or drug except under a written order of the medical officer specifying the nature and quantity and the name of the prisoner for whose use it is ordered.

(2) A prisoner shall not be allowed to smoke or have in his possession any tobacco except in accordance with such orders as may be given by the governor.

Clothing

84. (1) A prisoner shall wear clothing adequate for warmth and health in accordance with a scale approved by the Secretary of State (including any special clothing which the governor considers is required for any particular work or activity), and shall be provided with such clothing except to the extent that he provides his own clothing under paragraph (3).

(2) All clothing shall be clean and kept in proper condition; facilities shall be available for items to be changed as often as is necessary for the maintenance of health and hygiene.

(3) A prisoner may provide his own clothing except to the extent that -

(a) his own clothing is required for the purposes of justice; or

(b) his own clothing is prohibited under paragraph (4); or

(c) the governor considers that special clothing is required for any particular work or activity.

(4) The governor may prohibit clothing of any particular description or any particular item of clothing if he considers that the wearing of that clothing or item would be prejudicial to security, good order or discipline.

(5) Where such clothing as is provided under paragraph (1) is worn by a prisoner who is required to be taken in custody to court, it shall be such as does not indicate that he is a prisoner.

Medical officer

85. (1) The medical officer of a prison shall be responsible for the general care of prisoners' health.

(2) In the absence of the medical officer, his duties shall be performed by a registered medical practitioner approved by the chief medical officer and the Secretary of State.

(3) Arrangements shall be made at every prison to ensure that at all times a registered medical officer is either present at the prison or is able to attend the prison without delay in cases of urgency.

Duties of a medical officer

86. (1) The medical officer shall uphold the rules and regulations of the prison and shall support the governor.

(2) The medical officer shall report to the chief medical officer on, and inform the governor of, anything in the prison or the treatment of prisoners which appears to him to require consideration on medical grounds.

(3) The medical officer shall advise the governor on the hygiene of the prisoners, including the suitability and cleanliness of their clothing and bedding, and on the hygiene of the prison generally so far as he is able to do so.

(4) The medical officer shall every day see those prisoners who complain of illness and shall report to the governor in writing on their fitness for work.

(5) The medical officer shall be told at once if a prisoner appears to be seriously ill, and shall ensure that the prisoner is attended as soon as possible.

(6) Where a prisoner is thought to be a possible suicide risk by a governor, officer or other person employed in the prison they shall inform the medical officer and he shall consider whether any medical treatment is necessary.

(7) The medical officer shall give written directions for separating from other prisoners any prisoner whose health makes such separation advisable in his own interest or that of other prisoners.

(8) The medical officer shall at least once every day visit every prisoner under restraint, confined to a room or in cellular confinement, or any other prisoner to whom his attention is specifically directed.

(9) The medical officer shall not apply any painful tests to a prisoner for the purpose of detecting malingering or for any other purpose except with the permission of the board of visitors.

Medical records and statistics

87. (1) The medical officer shall record the condition of every sick prisoner, the nature of his disease, the medicines and the diet provided and any other treatment which he may order.

(2) The medical officer shall keep such statistical records and provide such statistical returns as the Secretary of State may direct relevant to his duties as a medical officer.

(3) The medical officer shall, as soon as possible after 31st March in each year, submit a report to the Secretary of State concerning

such matters relative to his duties during the year as the Secretary of State may direct.

Special medical reports

88. (1) When the medical officer believes that a prisoner's health is likely to be injuriously affected by continued imprisonment, or any conditions of imprisonment, he shall report the circumstances to the governor and to the chief medical officer for the information of the Secretary of State.

(2) The medical officer shall pay attention to any prisoner whose mental condition appears to require it and where appropriate make any special arrangements which appear necessary for his supervision or care.

(3) The medical officer shall inform the governor and the chief medical officer if he suspects that any prisoner is dangerously ill or has suicidal intentions, and the prisoner shall be placed under special observation.

(4) The medical officer may, with the approval of the chief medical officer, call another member of the medical profession or a member of an associated profession into consultation.

Operations

89. Except in urgent circumstances no major surgical procedures shall be performed in the prison.

PART X

WOMEN PRISONERS

Custody

90. (1) Women prisoners shall be held in separate accommodation.

(2) Prisoners of both sexes may participate together in work, education or other approved activities subject to the approval of the governor.

(3) Nothing in this rule shall unnecessarily deprive prisoners of the benefit of association with other persons.

Regimes

91. (1) In the provision of work, education, recreation, or privileges the governor may provide a different regime for women prisoners from that available to male prisoners.

(2) This rule does not permit any discrimination which would be unlawful but for the fact that it took place in a prison.

Pregnancy, confinement and babies

92. (1) Where a female prisoner is pregnant on committal and her confinement is expected to take place before the end of her sentence, she shall, if possible, be temporarily removed from the prison to a suitable hospital for the confinement and for any period following delivery which the medical officer considers necessary.

(2) The Secretary of State shall be notified of any such impending confinement and may thereupon direct removal of the prisoner under such conditions, if any, as he thinks fit.

(3) The Secretary of State may, subject to any conditions he thinks fit, permit a female prisoner to have her baby with her in prison and everything necessary for the baby's maintenance and care be provided there.

PART XI

PERSONS ORDERED TO BE DETAINED IN A YOUNG OFFENDERS CENTRE

Modifications to these rules

93. The following words shall be substituted in Rule 2 and throughout Parts II to X and XII to XVI of these rules as they apply to those requires to be detained in a young offenders centre -

(a) 'inmate' for 'prisoner';

(b) 'centre' for 'prison';

(c) 'visiting committee' for 'board of visitors';

(d) 'confinement room' for 'cellular confinement'.

Initial transfer to centre

94. (1) Where a person has been ordered to be detained in a centre he may be kept in custody in a prison other than a centre until arrangements can be made for a transfer to a centre.

(2) An inmate shall not be kept in prison under this rule for longer than 72 hours.

(3) While in custody in such a prison an inmate shall, so far as possible, be kept separate from other prisoners, but an inmate may associate with prisoners for work, education and exercise and for other purposes if otherwise he would be deprived of the benefits of association.

Disciplinary awards

95. (1) Rules 39(1) and 40(2) shall not apply to inmates of a young offenders centre.

(2) The governor may, subject to rules 40 and 41, make one of the following awards for an offence against discipline -

(a) caution;

(b) loss of remission for a period not exceeding 14 days;

(c) stoppage of earnings for a period not exceeding 14 days;

(d) stoppage of any privileges other than earnings, for a period not exceeding 28 days or 60 days in the case of evening association;

(e) exclusion from associated work for a period not exceeding 14 days;

(f) confinement to room for a period not exceeding 3 days.

(3) Where a charge is referred to the Secretary of State under rule 40(1) he shall, unless he delegates his powers under rule 40(4), inquire into the charge and, if he is satisfied that the offence has been committed, may make one or more of the following awards -

(a) caution;

(b) loss of remission;

(c) stoppage of earnings for a period not exceeding 28 days;

(d) stoppage of any or all privileges other than earnings, for a period not exceeding 56 days or 90 days in the case of evening association;

(e) exclusion from associated work for a period not exceeding 28 days;

(f) confinement to room for a period not exceeding 7 days or, where the inmate is found guilty of mutiny or incitement to mutiny or of assault of an officer, not exceeding 14 days.

(4) Subject to paragraph (5), where a person ordered to be detained in a young offenders centre is kept in custody in a prison under rule 92, any disciplinary award made under these rules in respect of any offence against discipline committed by him while in prison custody shall have effect as if made under this rule to the extent (if any) that the award has not been exhausted at the time of such transfer.

(5) No award shall have effect by virtue of paragraph (4) to the extent, if any, that the award made was more severe than could, at the time it was made, have been made under this rule.

Recreation

96. (1) Rule 55 shall not apply to inmates of a young offenders centre.

(2) Subject to paragraph (3) inmates shall regularly be given such physical recreation, training and exercise as required to promote health and physical well-being.

(3) The medical officer may on medical grounds, modify physical recreation, training or exercise or exempt an inmate from any or all of these.

PART XII

UNTRIED PRISONERS

General

97. This part shall apply to any person (in these rules referred to as "an untried prisoner") committed to prison for safe custody in any of the following circumstances -

>(a) on his commital for trial for any indictable offence;

>(b) pending the preliminary investigation or inquiry into an indictable offence by a magistrates court or pending the hearing of a complaint;

>(c) awaiting sentence or pending inquiries after a conviction; or

>(d) being held in lawful custody other than on conviction or where rule 107 applies.

(2) The treatment of untried prisoners shall be such as to recognise not only the governor's duty to ensure the course of justice but also their status as persons who have not been convicted of any offence.

Photographing and measuring

98. An untried prisoner shall not be photographed or measured while in prison except with the authority of the Secretary of State.

Separation from other prisoners

99. (1) Untried prisoners shall be kept out of contact with other prisoners as far as this can reasonably be done.

(2) Nothing in this rule shall require a prisoner to be deprived unduly of the society of other persons.

Legal assistance

100. (1) An untried prisoner shall receive -

>(a) all possible assistance with any application which he may wish to make to be released on bail; and

(b) all possible assistance and facilities to enable him to exercise his legal rights in connection with his trial.

(2) A confidential written communication prepared as instructions for the legal adviser of an untried prisoner may be delivered with seal unbroken to a messenger authorised, in writing, by the legal adviser to receive it, unless the governor has reason to suppose that it contains matter not relating to such instructions.

Contact with relatives and others

101. (1) An untried prisoner shall be assisted in maintaining close links with his relatives and friends, and in continuing as far as possible to deal with matters relating to employment, housing and any legitimate business.

(2) To this end he may send and receive as many letters and may receive as many visits as he wishes within such limits and subject to such conditions as the Secretary of State may direct, either generally or in a particular case.

(3) Subject to paragrpah (2) and rule 97(2), an untried prisoner shall be treated as any other prisoner for the purpose of receiving letters and visits.

Accommodation and hygiene

102. (1) An untried prisoner shall if possible be accomodated in a single cell, but if he expresses a wish to share a cell his preference shall be taken into account.

(2) An untried prisoner shall if possible have daily access to a bath or shower, opportunities for frequent changes of clothes, and be provided with the necessary means to keep his cell clean.

Daily activities

103. (1) Subject to proper requirements of safe custody and good order untried prisoners shall be unlocked each day for such period as the governor or the Secretary of State may direct; different periods may apply in different prisons and to different prisoners or classes of prisoners.

(2) Untried prisoners shall if possible have the option of eating in association or in their cells.

(3) Untried prisoners shall not be required to work, but shall have reasonable opportunities for access to purposeful activities including education and library books.

(4) An untried prisoner may, at the discretion of the governor, have supplied to him at his own expense books, newspapers, writing materials and other means of occupation.

(5) Where an untried prisoner works at his own request, he shall be allowed earnings under arrangements made in accordance with rule 51(10) of these rules.

Application of prisoner's money

104. (1) Any money which an untried prisoner has at a prison may be applied to the purpose of making special provision for him in cases where the prisoner is, by these rules, required to make any payment in respect of such provision.

(2) An untried prisoner may spend as much private cash as he wishes to purchase items which he is allowed to have in his possession.

Appearance and health

105. (1) An untried prisoner shall, so far as is practicable, maintain his external appearance as on committal and shall shave or be shaved as necessary for this purpose.

(2) Notwithstanding the provisions of paragraph (1) the medical officer may direct that an untried prisoner's hair be cut for the sake of health and cleanliness.

(3) If an untried prisoner desires the attendance of a registered medical practitioner or dentist, and will pay any expense incurred, the governor shall, if he is satisfied that there are reasonable grounds for the request and unless the Secretary of State otherwise directs, allow him to be visited and treated by that practitioner or dentist in consultation with the medical officer.

Property

106. (1) The governor may, on the application of an untried prisoner, allow him, so far as is consistent with security and the good order of the prison, to have in his cell any articles which were in his possession at the time of his arrest and are not required for the purposes of justice or reasonably suspected of forming part of property improperly acquired by him.

(2) No article, whether of clothing or any other kind, shall be received into prison for an untried prisoner until it has been examined, any article which appears likely to be used for an improper purpose may be refused by the governor.

(3) An article may also be refused by the governor if it is not of an essential nature and if its addition to the items which the prisoner already has in his possession would make the prisoner's cell unduly cluttered or unreasonably difficult to search.

(4) An untried prisoner shall not sell or transfer to any other person any article allowed to be introduced for his use; and any prisoner offending against this rule may be prohibited from procuring any such article for such a period as the Secretary of State considers proper.

PART XIII

PRISONERS COMMITTED FOR CONTEMPT, ETC

Letters and visits

107. Rules 100 and 101 shall have effect in relation to a prisoner committed or attached for contempt of court, or for failing to do or abstain from doing anything required to be done or left undone, as it has effect in relation to an untried prisoner.

Association

108. Such prisoners shall be treated as a separate class for the purposes of rule 9 but prisoners may be permitted to associate with any other class of prisoners if they are willing to do so.

Remission

109. A person detained in prison for a stated term of more than 5 days on committal or attachment for contempt of court shall, for the purposes of rule 30, be treated as serving a sentence of imprisonment for a like term.

PART XIV

GENRAL RULES RELATING TO OFFICERS

General duties of officers

110. (1) Every officer shall conform to these rules and whatever rules and regulations may be in force in the prison and shall assist and support the governor in maintaining them.

(2) Every officer shall perform his duties conscientiously and shall be courteous towards other officers, staff and members of the public.

(3) An officer shall obey the lawful instructions of the governor.

(4) An officer shall inform the governor promptly of any breach of these rules or any abuse or impropriety.

Contact with prisoners

111. (1) An officer shall ensure that in his dealings with prisoners that he is courteous and that his conduct is correct and proper at all times.

(2) An officer shall inform the governor promptly of any prisoner who appears to be unwell, or whose behaviour or attitude indicates, in the opinion of the officer, that he may be suicidal or otherwise require further attention or advice.

(3) Except with the permission of the governor, an officer shall not discuss his duties or any matter of discipline or prison arrangements within the hearing of a prisoner.

(4) No officer shall take part in any business or pecuniary transaction with, or on behalf of, a prisoner without the permission of the Secretary of State.

(5) Except with the permission of the governor, no officer shall bring in or take out, or attempt to bring in or take out, or

knowingly allow to be brought in or taken out, to or from a prisoner, or deposit in any place with intent that it shall come into the possession of a prisoner, any article whatsoever.

Contact with ex-prisoners

112. (1) If a former prisoner or a relative or friend of a prisoner or former prisoner communicates or attempts to communicate with an officer, the officer shall inform the governor.

(2) No officer shall communicate with a former prisoner or a relative or friend of a prisoner or former prisoner without the permission of the governor.

Gratuities

113. (1) An officer shall not receive any unauthorised fee, gratuity or other consideration in connection with his office.

(2) If an officer is offered a fee, gratuity or any consideration by any person he will inform the governor.

Contracts

114. Except with the permission of the Secretary of State, an officer shall not, directly or indirectly, have any interest in any contract or tender connected with the prison or receive a fee, gratuity or any other consideration from any contractor, or from any person tendering, or any other person whatever in connection with any such contract or tender.

Communications to press, etc.

115. (1) Except with the permission of the Secretary of State, an officer shall not directly or indirectly communicate to a representative of the press, television or radio or any other person matters which he has come to know in the course of his official duties.

(2) An officer shall not, without the permission of the Secretary of State, publish any matter or make any public pronouncement relating to the administration of any prison or to any of its prisoners.

PART XV

SPECIAL RULES RELATING TO GOVERNORS

Status of governor

116. (1) The governor shall be in command of the prison.

(2) The governor shall be responsible for the safe custody of all prisoners until they are discharged from his custody by the expiration of their sentence or by order of a court or by Royal Warrant or by order of the Secretary of State.

(3) The governor shall be responsible for prisoners' treatment according to law, for the safeguarding of their rights and for the maintenance of discipline in prison.

(4) Subject to any direction from the Secretary of State, the governor shall have authority over all officers and employees on the staff of the prison.

(5) The governor shall ensure the safe custody and proper disposal or use of all monies, equipment and materials in the prison and shall keep whatever records and accounts are required by direction of the Secretary of State.

Delegation by governor

117. (1) In a prison where a deputy governor has been appointed, the deputy governor shall, in the absence of the governor, act for him.

(2) Subject to paragraph (1), the prison shall in the governor's absence, be in the charge of an officer approved by the Secretary of State and the officer so approved shall, at such a time, be competent to perform and shall perform any duty required of the governor.

(3) Subject to the Act and to the provisions of Part IV of these rules and any directions by the Secretary of State, the governor may delegate to another officer any of his functions under these rules.

Powers and duties relating to officers

118. (1) The governor shall superintend the conduct of the officers under his authority.

(2) The governor may suspend an officer if there is prima facie evidence of misconduct and shall, without delay, report the matter fully to the Secretary of State and shall carry out any directions given by the Secretary of State.

(3) The governor shall deal with offences against discipline as empowered by the Secretary of State under any code of conduct made under rule 6.

(4) The governor shall record all his orders relating to the management and discipline of the prison and shall have such orders communicated to the proper officers.

(5) The governor shall keep such records of officers' conduct as the Secretary of State may determine.

(6) The governor shall forward without delay any report or complaint which an officer wishes to make to the Secretary of State and may add any reports he feels appropriate.

(7) The governor shall -

(a) make available, as he considers appropriate, to all officers and other staff circulars from the Secretary of State and other documents relating to their duties, rights and responsibilities including any code of conduct made under rule 6; and

(b) also ensure that such officers and staff have adequate opportunity to acquaint themselves with the contents of these documents.

Duties in relation to medical officer

119. Without prejudice to his other duties under these rules the governor shall-

(a) without delay draw the attention of the medical officer to any prisoner whose physical or mental condition appears to require attention;

(b) at once notify the medical officer of any prisoner who is sick or any officer who is in need of urgent medical attention;

(c) provide the medical officer daily with a list of prisoners who have reported sick;

(d) provide the medical officer with a list of prisoners under punishment or confined in special cells;

(e) support the medical officer in his care of prisoners' health and to this end give as full effect as is practicable to recommendations by the medical officer.

Duties in relation to medical welfare of prisoners and to inquests

120. (1) The governor shall, without delay, report to the Secretary of State-

> (a) any case in which the medical officer believes that a prisoner's mental state is becoming impaired by continual imprisonment;

> (b) in any case in which the medical officer believes that a prisoner's life will be endangered by further imprisonment, or that a prisoner will not survive his sentence or is totally or permanently unfit for the discipline of the prison.

(2) The governor shall ensure that proper arrangements are made for the safe custody of sick prisoners and shall visit the prison hospital daily to see all prisoners who have been admitted there.

(3) The governor shall inform the appropriate chaplain when a prisoner recorded as of his denomination is dangerously ill, and shall allow such a prisoner to see any minister of religion whom the prisoner wishes to see.

(4) The governor shall satisfy himself that all officers and other staff who may be in contact with prisoners are aware of the proper procedures for seeking to identify, and for dealing with prisoners who for whatever reason may be regarded as suicide risks, and in

consultation with the medical officer ensure as far as possible that these procedures operate effectively.

(5) The governor shall apply to the coroner holding an inquest on a prisoner who has died while in his custody the name of any prisoner who claims to be able and willing to give relevant evidence.

(6) The governor shall attend any inquest following the death of a prisoner in his custody, or arrange for an appropriate officer to do so, and shall report to the Secretary of State on the findings of the inquest.

Other duties of the governor

121. (1) The governor shall keep a journal in which he shall record, with the time thereof, any matter or occurrences of a significant or unusual nature.

(2) The governor shall provide such statistical or other information as the Secretary of State may direct, whether for the purpose of an annual report required by section 5 of the Act or otherwise.

(3) The provisions of rules 112, 113 and 114 shall have effect in relation to governors as well as to other officers.

PART XVI

POWERS AND DUTIES OF BOARDS OF VISITORS

Appointment of members

122. (1) The members of a board of visitors appointed under section 10 of the Act shall hold office for a period of 3 years, or such less period as the Secretary of State may direct.

(2) Any person interested in any contract for the supply of goods or services shall not be a member of the board of visitors for that prison.

(3) The Secretary of State may terminate the appointment of a member if he is satisfied that-

(a) he has failed to perform his duties satisfactorily,

(b) he is by reason of physical or mental illness, or for any other reason, incapable of carrying out his duties; or

(c) he has been convicted of a criminal offence, or his conduct has been such that it is not fitting that he should remain a member.

(4) The first business at the first meeting of a board of visitors after appointment shall be the election of a chairman.

(5) The chairman of a board of visitors may be elected for the whole term of office of the board, or, at the discretion of the board, he may be elected annually.

(6) The board may elect, for such term of office as it decides, a deputy chairman who shall preside at any meeting at which the chairman is not present.

(7) The members shall continue in office until the date of the first meeting of their successors.

Proceedings of the board

123. (1) The board shall meet at the prison once a month to discharge its functions under these rules.

(2) The quorum at a meeting of the board shall be three except as provided under rule 125(3).

(3) The powers of the board shall not be affected by vacancies in its membership or any defect in the appointment of a member.

(4) The board shall keep minutes of its proceedings and a copy of the minutes shall be sent to the Secretary of State as soon as is practicable after any meeting.

(5) At each meeting of the board a rota shall be arranged to ensure that the prison is visited by at least two visitors before the board's next meeting; these arrangements shall be made in such a way as to ensure that all parts of the prison are visited at reasonable intervals.

(6) A member visiting a prison shall report on his visit to the board.

General duties of the board

124. (1) The board of visitors for a prison shall satisfy itself as to -

(a) the treatment of prisoners including provision for their health care and other welfare while in prison;

(b) the facilities available to prisoners to allow them to make purposeful use of their time; and

(c) the cleanliness and adequacy of prison premises.

(2) The board shall enquire into and report upon any matter which the Secretary of State refers to it.

(3) The board shall direct the attention of the governor to any matter which it considers calls for his attention, and shall report to the Secretary of State any matter which it considers should be reported to him.

(4) The board shall inform the Secretary of State immediately of any abuse which comes to its knowledge in connection with the prison.

(5) In the exercise of any of its powers, a board shall satisfy itself, in consultation with the governor, that the exercise of the power will not-

(a) undermine the security and good order of the prison;

(b) prejudice the efficient operation of the prison; or

(c) prevent the proper treatment of prisoners.

Adjudication procedure by boards

125. (1) The board shall inquire into any alleged offence against discipline where the Secretary of State has delegated to it his powers under rule 40.

(2) The board shall record in its minutes each such case and the award made and shall report thereon to the Secretary of State.

(3) The powers of the board under this rule shall be exercised at a special meeting consisting of not less than 2 members or more than 5 members.

Visits by board members

126. (1) Members of the board shall have free access at any time to all parts of the prison to which they are appointed, and to all prisoners and may interview any prisoner out of sight and hearing of prison staff.

(2) In exercising their rights under this rule, members shall take into consideration the matters referred to in rule 123(5).

(3) The governor shall allow the board reasonable access to any of the records of the prison, but this shall not entitle the board to see records which the governor must keep secret under a duty of confidentiality.

Annual report

127. The board shall, as soon as possible after 31st March in any year , report to the Secretary of State on all or any of their year's duties under these rules together with any advice or suggestions they may wish to make.

Northern Ireland Office

P.B.B. Mayhew

10th January 1995
Principal

One of Her Majesty's

Secretaries of State

SCHEDULE

Prisons

Belfast

Maghaberry

Magilligan

Maze

Annex B - European Convention on Human Rights

COUNCIL OF EUROPE

CONVENTION FOR THE PROTECTION OF HUMAN RIGHTS AND FUNDAMENTAL FREEDOMS

The governments signatory hereto, being Members of the Council of Europe,

Considering the Universal Declaration of Human Rights proclaimed by the General Assembly of the United Nations on 10th December 1948;

Considering that this Declaration aims at securing the universal and effective recognition and observance of the rights therein declared;

Considering that the aim of the Council of Europe is the achievement of greater unity between its Members and that one of the methods by which that aim is to be pursued is the maintenance and further realisation of human rights and fundamental freedoms;

Reaffirming their profound belief in those fundamental freedoms which are the foundation of justice and peace in the world and are best maintained on the one hand by an effective political democracy and on the other by a common understanding and observance of the Human Rights upon which they depend;

Being resolved, as the governments of European countries which are like-minded and have a common heritage of political traditions, ideals, freedoms and the rule of law, to take the first steps for the collective enforcement of certain of the rights stated in the Universal Declaration;

Have agreed as follows:

Article 1

The High Contracting Parties shall secure to everyone within their jurisdiction the rights and freedoms defined in Section 1 of this Convention.

SECTION I

Article 2

1. Everyone's rights to life shall be protected by law. No one shall be deprived of his life intentionally save in the execution of a sentence of a court following his conviction of a crime for which this penalty is provided by law.

2. Deprivation of life shall not be regarded as inflicted in contravention of this Article when it results from the use of force which is no more than is absolutely necessary:

(a) in defence of any person from unlawful violence;

(b) in order to effect a lawful arrest or to prevent the escape of a person lawfully detained:

(c) in action lawfully taken for the purpose of quelling a riot or insurrection.

Article 3

No one shall be subjected to torture or to inhuman or degrading treatment or punishment.

Article 4

1. No one shall be held in slavery or servitude.

2. No one shall be required to perform forced or compulsory labour.

3. For the purpose of this Article the term "forced or compulsory labour" shall not include:

(a) any work required to be done in the ordinary course of detention imposed according to the provisions of Article 5 of this Convention or during conditional release from such detention;

(b) any service of a military character or, in case of conscientious objectors in countries where they are recognised, service exacted instead of compulsory military service;

(c) any service exacted in the case of an emergency or calamity threatening the life or well-being of the community;

(d) any work or service which forms part of normal civic obligations.

Article 5

1. Everyone has the right to liberty and security of person. No one shall be deprived of his liberty save in the following circumstances and in accordance with a procedure prescribed by law:

(a) the lawful detention of a person after conviction;

(b) the lawful arrest or detention of a person for non-compliance with the lawful order of a court or in order to secure the fulfilment of any obligation prescribed by law;

(c) the lawful arrest or detention of a person effected for the purpose of bringing him before the competent legal authority on reasonable suspicion of having committed an offence or when it is reasonably considered necessary to prevent his committing an offence or fleeing after having done so;

(d) the detention of a minor by lawful order for the purpose of educational supervision or his lawful detention for the purpose of bringing him before the competent legal authority;

(e) the lawful detention of persons for the prevention of the spreading of infectious diseases, of persons of unsound mind, alcoholics or drug addicts or vagrants;

(f) the lawful arrest or detention of a person to prevent his effecting an unauthorised entry into the country or of a person against whom action is being taken with a view to deportation or extradition.

2. Everyone who is arrested shall be informed promptly, in a language which he understands, of the reasons for his arrest and of any charge against him.

3. Everyone arrested or detained in accordance with the provisions of paragraph 1.c of this Article shall be brought promptly before a judge

or other officer authorised by law to exercise judicial power and shall be entitled to trial within a reasonable time or to release pending trial. Release may be conditioned by guarantees to appear for trial.

4. Everyone who is deprived of his liberty by arrest or detention shall be entitled to take proceedings by which the lawfulness of his detention shall be decided speedily by a court and his release ordered if the detention is not lawful.

5. Everyone who has been the victim of arrest or detention in contravention of the provisions of this Article shall have an enforceable right to compensation.

Article 6
1. In the determination of his civil rights and obligations or of any criminal charge against him, everyone is entitled to a fair and public hearing within a reasonable time by an independent and impartial tribunal established by law. Judgement shall be pronounced publicly but the press and public may be excluded from all or part of the trial in the interest of morals, public order or national security in a democratic society, where the interests of juveniles or the protection of the private life of the parties so require, or to the extent strictly necessary in the opinion of the court in special circumstances where publicity would prejudice the interests of justice.

2. Everyone charged with a criminal offence shall be presumed innocent until proved guilty according to law.

3. Everyone charged with a criminal offence has the following minimum rights :

(a) to be informed promptly, in a language which he understands and in detail, of the nature and cause of the accusation against him;

(b) to have adequate time and facilities for the preparation of his defence;

(c) to defend himself in person or through legal assistance of his own choosing or, if he has not sufficient means to pay for legal assistance, to be given it free when the interests of justice so require;

(d) to examine or have examined witnesses against him and to obtain the attendance and examination of witnesses on his behalf under the same conditions as witnesses against him:

(e) to have the free assistance of an interpreter if he cannot understand or speak the language used in court.

Article 7

1. No one shall be held guilty of any criminal offence on account of any act or omission which did not constitute a criminal offence under national or international law at the time when it was committed. Nor shall a heavier penalty be imposed than the one that was applicable at the time the criminal offence was committed.

2. This Article shall not prejudice the trial and punishment of any person for any act or omission which, at the time when it was committed, was criminal according to the general principles of law recognised by civilised nations.

Article 8

1. Everyone has the right to respect for his private and family life, his home and his correspondence.

2. There shall be no interference by a public authority with the exercise of this right except such as is in accordance with the law and is necessary in a democratic society in the interests of national security, public safety or the economic well-being of the country, for the prevention of disorder or crime, for the protection of health or morals, or for the protection of the rights and freedoms of others.

Article 9

1. Everyone has the right to freedom of thought, conscience and religion; this right includes freedom to change his religion or belief and freedom, either alone or in community with others and in public or private, to manifest his religion or belief, in worship, teaching, practice and observance.

2. Freedom to manifest one's religions or beliefs shall be subject only to such limitations as are prescribed by law and are necessary in a democratic society in the interests of public safety, for the protection of public order, health or morals, or for the protection of the rights and freedoms of others.

Article 10

1. Everyone has the right to freedom of expression. This right shall include freedom to hold opinions and to receive and impart information and ideas without interference by public authority and regardless of frontiers. This Article shall not prevent States from requiring the licensing of broadcasting, television or cinema enterprises.

2. The exercise of these freedoms, since it carries with it duties and responsibilities, may be subject to such formalities, conditions, restrictions or penalties as are prescribed by law and are necessary in a democratic society, in the interests of national security, territorial integrity or public safety, for the prevention of disorder or crime, for the protection of health and morals , for the protection of the reputation or rights of others, for preventing the disclosure of information received in confidence, or for maintaining the authority and impartiality of the judiciary.

Article 11

1. Everyone has the right to freedom of peaceful assembly and to freedom of association with others, including the right to form and to join trade unions for the protection of his interests.

2. No restrictions shall be placed on the exercise of these rights other than such as are prescribed by law and are necessary in a democratic society in the interests of national security or public safety, for the prevention of disorder or crime, for the protection of health or morals or for the protection of the rights and freedoms of others. This Article shall not prevent the imposition of lawful restrictions on the exercise of these rights by members of the armed forces, of the police or of the administration of the state.

Article 12

Men and women of marriageable age have the right to marry and found a family, according to the national laws governing the exercise of this right.

Article 13

Everyone whose rights and freedoms as set forth in this Convention are violated shall have an effective remedy before a national authority notwithstanding that the violation has been committed by persons acting in an official capacity.

Article 14

The enjoyment of the rights and freedoms set forth in this Convention shall be secured without discrimination on any ground such as sex, race, colour, language, religion, political or other opinion, national or social origin, association with a national minority, property, birth or other status.

Article 15

1. In time of war or any other public emergency threatening the life of the nation any High Contracting Party may take measures derogating from its obligations under this convention to the extent strictly required by the exigencies of the situation, provided that such measures are not inconsistent with its other obligations under international law.

2. No derogation from Article 2, except in respect of deaths resulting from lawful acts of war, or from Articles 3, 4 (paragraph 1) and 7 shall be made under this provision.

3.   Any High Contracting Party availing itself of this right of derogation shall keep the Secretary General of the Council of Europe fully informed of the measures which it has taken and the reasons therefor. It shall also inform the Secretary General of the Council of Europe when such measures have ceased to operate and the provisions of the Convention are again being fully executed.

Article 16

Nothing in Articles 10, 11 and 14 shall be regarded as preventing the High Contracting Parties from imposing restrictions on the political activity of aliens.

Article 17

Nothing in this Convention may be interpreted as implying for any State, group or person any right to engage in any activity or perform any act aimed at the destruction of any of the rights and freedoms set forth herein or at their limitation to a greater extent than is provided for in the Convention.

Article 18

The restrictions permitted under this Convention to the said rights and freedoms shall not be applied for any purpose other than those for which they have been prescribed.

SECTION II

Article 19

To ensure the observance of the engagements undertaken by the High Contracting Parties in the convention, there shall be set up:

(a) A European Commission of Human Rights, hereinafter referred to as "the Commission";

(b) A European Court of Human Rights, hereinafter referred to as "the Court".

SECTION III

Article 20

1. The Commission shall consist of a number of members equal to that of the High Contracting Parties. No two members of the Commission may be nationals of the same State.

2. The Commission shall sit in plenary session. It may, however, set up Chambers, each composed of at least seven members. The Chambers may examine petitions submitted under Article 25 of this Convention which can be dealt with on the basis of established case law or which raise no serious question affecting the interpretation or application of the Convention. Subject to this restriction and to the provisions of paragraph 5 of this Article, the Chambers shall exercise all the powers conferred on the Commission by the Convention.

The member of the Commission elected in respect of a High Contracting Party against which a petition has been lodged shall have the right to sit on a Chamber to which that petition has been referred.

3. The Commission may set up Committees, each composed of at least three members, with the power, exercisable by a unanimous vote, to declare inadmissible or strike from its list of cases a petition submitted under Article 25, when such a decision can be taken without further examination.

4. A Chamber or Committee may at any time relinquish jurisdiction in favour of the plenary Commission, which may also order the transfer to it of any petition referred to a Chamber or Committee.

5. Only the plenary Commission can exercise the following powers:

> (a) the examination of applications submitted under Article 24;

> (b) the bringing of a case before the Court in accordance with Article 48a:

> (c) the drawing up of rules of procedure in accordance with Article 36.

Article 21

1. The members of the Commission shall be elected by the Committee of Ministers by an absolute majority of votes, from a list of names drawn up by the Bureau of the Consultative Assembly; each group of the Representatives of the High Contracting Parties in the Consultative Assembly shall put forward three candidates, of whom two at least shall be its nationals.

2. As far as applicable, the same procedure shall be followed to complete the Commission in the event of other States subsequently becoming parties to this Convention, and in filling casual vacancies.

3. The candidates shall be of high moral character and must either possess the qualifications required for appointment to high judicial office or be persons of recognised competence in national or international law.

Article 22

1. The members of the Commission shall be elected for a period of six years. They may be re-elected. However, of the members elected at the first election, the terms of seven members shall expire at the end of three years.

2. The members whose terms are to expire at the end of the initial period of three years shall be chosen by lot by the Secretary General of the Council of Europe immediately after the first election has been completed.

3. In order to ensure that, as far as possible, one half of the membership of the Commission shall be renewed every three years, the Committee of Ministers may decide, before proceeding to any subsequent election, that the term or terms of office of one or more members to be elected shall be for a period other than six years but not more than nine and not less than three years.

4. In cases where more than one term of office is involved and the Committee of Ministers applies the preceding paragraph, the allocation of the terms of office shall be effected by the drawing of lots by the Secretary General, immediately after the election.

5. A member of the Commission elected to replace a member whose term of office has not expired shall hold office for the remainder of his predecessor's term.

6. The members of the Commission shall hold office until replaced. After having been replaced, they shall continue to deal with such cases as they already have under consideration.

Article 23

The members of the Commission shall sit on the Commission in their individual capacity. During their term of office they shall not hold any position which is incompatible with their independence and impartiality as members of the Commission or the demands of this office.

Article 24

Any High Contracting Party may refer to the Commission, through the Secretary General of the Council of Europe, any alleged breach of the provisions of the Convention by another High Contracting Party.

Article 25

1. The Commission may receive petitions addressed to the Secretary General of the Council of Europe from any person, non-governmental organisation or group of individuals claiming to be the victim of a violation by one of the High Contracting Parties of the rights set forth in this Convention, provided that the High Contracting Party against which the complaint has been lodged has declared that it recognises the competence of the Commission to receive such petitions. Those of the High Contracting Parties who have made such a declaration undertake not to hinder in any way the effective exercise of this right.

2. Such declarations may be made for a specific period.

3. The declarations shall be deposited with the Secretary General of the Council of Europe who shall transmit copies thereof to the High Contracting Parties and publish them.

4. The Commission shall only exercise the powers provided for in this Article when at least six High Contracting Parties are bound by declarations made in accordance with the preceding paragraphs.

Article 26

The Commission may only deal with the matter after all domestic remedies have been exhausted, according to the generally recognised rules of international law, and within a period of six months from the date on which the final decision was taken.

Article 27

1. The Commission shall not deal with any petition submitted under Article 25 which:

> (a) is anonymous, or

> (b) is substantially the same as a matter which has already been examined by the Commission or has already been submitted to another procedure of international investigation or settlement and if it contains no relevant new information.

2. The Commission shall consider inadmissible any petition submitted under Article 25 which it considers incompatible with the provision of the present Convention, manifestly ill-founded, or an abuse of the right to petition.

3. The Commission shall reject any petition referred to it which it considers inadmissible under Article 26.

In addition there are a number of further provisions to the Convention, none of which relate to imprisonment.

ANNEX C - EUROPEAN PRISON RULES

The European Prison Rules

COUNCIL OF EUROPE 1987

PREAMBLE

The purpose of these rules are:

a. to establish a range of minimum standards for all those aspects of prison administration that are essential to humane conditions and positive treatment in modern and progressive systems;

b. to serve as a stimulus to prison administrations to develop policies and management style and practice based on good contemporary principles of purpose and equity;

c. to encourage in prison staffs professional attitudes that reflect the important social and moral qualities of their work and to create conditions in which they can optimise their own performance to the benefit of society in general, the prisoners in their care and their own vocational satisfaction;

d. to provide realistic basic criteria against which prison administrations and those responsible for inspecting the conditions and management of prisons can make valid judgements of performance and measure progress towards higher standards.

It is emphasised that the rules do not constitute a model system and that, in practice, many European prison services are already operating well above many of the standards laid out in the rules and that others are striving, and will continue to strive to do so. Wherever there are difficulties or practical problems to be overcome in the application of the rules, the Council of Europe has the machinery and the expertise available to assist with advice and the fruits of the experience of the various prison administrations within its sphere.

In these rules, renewed emphasis has been placed on the precepts of human dignity, the commitment of prison administrations to humane and positive treatments, the importance of staff roles and effective modern management approaches. They are set out to provide ready reference, encouragement and guidance to those who are working at all levels of prison administration. The explanatory memorandum that accompanies the rules is intended to ensure the understanding, acceptance and flexibility that are necessary to achieve the highest realistic level of implementation beyond the basic standards.

Part 1

THE BASIC PRINCIPLES

1. The deprivation of liberty shall be effected in material and moral conditions which ensure respect for human dignity and are in conformity with these rules.

2. The rules shall be applied impartially. There shall be no discrimination on grounds of race, colour, sex, language, religion, political or other opinion, national or social origin, birth, economic or other status. The religious beliefs and moral precepts of the group to which a prisoner belongs shall be respected.

3. The purposes of the treatment of persons in custody shall be such as to sustain their health and self respect and, so far as the length of sentence permits, to develop their sense of responsibility and encourage those attitudes and skills that will assist them to return to society with the best chance of leading law-abiding and self-supporting lives after their release.

4. There shall be regular inspections of penal institutions and services by qualified and experienced inspectors appointed by a competent authority. Their task shall be, in particular, to monitor whether and to what extent these institutions are administered in accordance with existing laws and regulations, the objectives of the prison services and the requirements of these rules.

5. The protection of the individual rights of prisoners with special regard to the legality of the execution of detention measures shall be secured by means of a control carried out, according to national rules, by a judicial authority or other duly constituted body authorised to visit the prisoners and not belonging to the prison administration.

6. 1.   These rules shall be made readily available to staff in the national languages;

   2.   They shall also be available to prisoners in the same languages and in other languages so far as is reasonable and practicable.

RECEPTION AND REGISTRATION

7. 1.   No person shall be received in an institution without a valid commitment order.

   2.   The essential details of the commitment and reception shall immediately be recorded.

8.   In every place where persons are imprisoned a complete and secure record of the following information shall be kept concerning each prisoner received:

   a.   information concerning the identity of the prisoner;

   b.   the reasons for commitment and the authority therefor;

   c.   the day and hour of admission and release.

9.   Reception arrangements shall conform with the basic principles of the rules and shall assist prisoners to resolve their urgent personal problems.

10. 1.   As soon as possible after reception, full reports and relevant information about the personal situation and training programme of each prisoner with a sentence of suitable length in preparation for ultimate release shall be drawn up and submitted to the director for information or approval as appropriate.

   2.   Such reports shall always include reports by a medical officer and the personnel in direct charge of the prisoner concerned.

   3.   The reports and information concerning prisoners shall be maintained with due regard to confidentiality on an individual basis, regularly kept up to date and only accessible to authorised persons.

THE ALLOCATION AND CLASSIFICATION OF PRISONERS

11. 1. In allocating prisoners to different institutions and regimes, due account shall be taken of their judicial and legal situation (untried or convicted prisoner, first offender or habitual offender, short sentence or long sentence), of the special requirements of their treatment, of their medical needs, their sex and age.

    2. Males and females shall in principle be detained separately, although they may participate together in organised activities as   part of an established treatment programme.

    3. In principle, untried prisoners shall be detained separately from convicted prisoners unless they consent to being accommodated or involved together in organised activities beneficial to them.

    4. Young prisoners shall be detained under conditions which as far as possible protect them from harmful influences and which take account of the needs of their particular age.

12. The purposes of classification or re-classification of prisoners shall be:

    a. to separate from others those prisoners who , by reasons of their criminal records or their personality, are likely to benefit from that or who may exercise a bad influence.

    b. to assist in allocating prisoners to facilitate their treatment and social resettlement taking into account the management and security requirements.

13. So far as possible separate institutions or separate sections of an institution shall be used to facilitate the management of different treatment regimes or the allocation of specific categories of prisoners.

ACCOMMODATION

14. 1.   Prisoners shall normally be lodged during the night in individual cells except in cases where it is considered that there are advantages in sharing accommodation with other prisoners.

2.   Where accommodation is shared it shall be occupied by prisoners suitable to associate with others in those conditions. There shall be supervision by night, in keeping with the nature of the institution.

15.   The accommodation provided for prisoners, and in particular all sleeping accommodation, shall meet the requirements of health and hygiene, due regard being paid to climatic conditions and especially the cubic content of air, a reasonable amount of space, lighting, heating and ventilation.

16.   In all places where prisoners are required to live or work:

   a.   The windows shall be large enough to enable the prisoners *inter alia* to read or work by natural light in normal conditions. They shall be so constructed that they can allow the entrance of fresh air except where there is an adequate air conditioning system. Moreover, the windows shall, with due regard to security requirements, present in their size, location and construction as normal an appearance as possible;

   b.   artificial light shall satisfy recognised technical standards.

17.   The sanitary installations and arrangement for access shall be adequate to enable every prisoner to comply with the needs of nature when necessary and in clean and decent conditions.

18.   Adequate bathing and showering installations shall be provided so that every prisoner may be enabled and required to have a bath or shower, at a temperature suitable to the climate, as frequently as necessary for general hygiene according to season and geographical region, but at least one a week. Wherever possible there should be free access at all reasonable times.

19.   All parts of an institution shall be properly maintained and kept clean at all times.

PERSONAL HYGIENE

20. Prisoners shall be required to keep their persons clean, and to this end they shall be provided with water and with such toilet articles as are necessary for health and cleanliness.

21. For reasons of health and in order that prisoners may maintain a good appearance and preserve their self-respect, facilities shall be provided for the proper care of the hair and beard, and men shall be enabled to shave regularly.

CLOTHING AND BEDDING

22. 1. Prisoners who are not allowed to wear their own clothing shall be provided with an outfit of clothing suitable for the climate and adequate to keep them in good health. Such clothing shall in no manner be degrading or humiliating.

    2. All clothing shall be clean and kept in proper condition. Under-clothing shall be changed and washed as often as necessary for the maintenance of hygiene.

    3. Whenever prisoners obtain permission to go outside the institution, they shall be allowed to wear their own clothing or other inconspicuous clothing.

23. On the admission of prisoners to an institution, adequate arrangements shall be made to ensure that their personal clothing is kept in good condition and fit for use.

24. Every prisoner shall be provided with a separate bed and separate and appropriate bedding which shall be kept in good order and changed often enough to ensure its cleanliness.

FOOD

25. 1. In accordance with the standards laid down by the health authorities, the administration shall provide the prisoners at the normal times with food which is suitably prepared and presented, and which satisfies in quality and quantity the standards of dietetics and modern hygiene and takes into account their age, health, the nature of their work, and so far as possible, religious or cultural requirements.

2. Drinking water shall be available to every prisoner.

MEDICAL SERVICES

26. 1. At every institution there shall be available the services of at least one qualified general practitioner. The medical services should be organised in close relation with the general health administration of the community or nation. They shall include a psychiatric service for the diagnosis and, in proper cases, the treatment of states of mental abnormality.

   2. Sick prisoners who require specialist treatment shall be transferred to specialised institutions or civil hospitals. Where hospital facilities are provided in an institution, their equipment, furnishings and pharmaceutical supplies shall be suitable for the medical care and treatment of sick prisoners, and there shall be a staff of suitably trained officers.

   3. The services of a qualified dental officer shall be available to every prisoner.

27. Prisoners may not be submitted to any experiments which may result in physical or moral injury.

28. 1. Arrangements shall be made wherever practicable for children to be born in a hospital outside the institution. However, unless special arrangements are made, there shall in penal institutions be the necessary staff and accommodation for the confinement and post-natal care of pregnant care of women. If a child is born in prison, this fact shall not be mentioned in the birth certificate.

   2. Where infants are allowed to remain in the institution with their mothers, special provision shall be made for a nursery staffed by qualified persons, where the infants shall be placed when they are not in the care of their mothers.

29. The medical officer shall see and examine every prisoner as soon as possible after admission and thereafter as necessary, with a view particularly to the discovery of physical or mental illness and the taking of all measures necessary for medical treatment; the segregation of prisoners suspected of infectious or contagious

conditions; the noting of physical or mental defects which might impede resettlement after release; and the determination of the fitness of every prisoner to work.

30. 1. The medical officer shall have the care of the physical and mental health of the prisoners and shall see, under the conditions and with a frequency consistent with medical standards, all sick prisoners, all who report illness or injury and any prisoner to whom attention is specially directed.

  2. The medical officer shall report to the director whenever it is considered that a prisoner's physical or mental health has been or will be adversely affected by continued imprisonment or by any condition of imprisonment.

31. 1. The medical officer or a competent authority shall regularly inspect and advise the director upon :

    a. the quantity, quality, preparation and serving of food and water;

    b. the hygiene and cleanliness of the institution and prisoners;

    c. the sanitation, heating, lighting and ventilation of the institution;

    d. the suitability and cleanliness of the prisoners' clothing and bedding.

  2. The director shall consider the reports and advice that the medical officer submits according to Rules 30, paragraph 2, and 31, paragraph 1, and, when in concurrence with the recommendations made, shall take immediate steps to give affect to those recommendations; if they are not within the director's competence or if the director does not concur with them, the director shall immediately submit a written report and the advice of the medical officer to higher authority.

32. The medical services of the institution shall seek to detect and shall treat any physical or mental illnesses or defects which may impede a prisoner's resettlement after release. All necessary medical, surgical and psychiatric services including those

available in the community shall be provided to the prisoner to that end.

DISCIPLINE AND PUNISHMENT

33. Discipline and order shall be maintained in the interests of safe custody, ordered community life and the treatment objectives of the institution.

34. 1. No prisoner shall be employed, in the service of the institution, in any disciplinary capacity.

    2. This rule shall not, however, impede the proper functioning of arrangements under which specified social, educational or sports activities or responsibilities are entrusted under supervision to prisoners who are formed into groups for the purposes of their participation in regime programmes.

35. The following shall be provided for and determined by the law or by the regulation of the competent authority:

    a. conduct constituting a disciplinary offence;

    b. the types and duration of punishment which may be imposed;

    c. the authority competent to impose such punishment;

    d. access to, and the authority of, the appellate process.

36. 1. No prisoner shall be punished except in accordance with the terms of such law or regulation and never twice for the same act.

    2. Reports of misconduct shall be presented promptly to the competent authority who shall decide on them without undue delay.

    3. No prisoner shall be punished unless informed of the alleged offence and given the proper opportunity of presenting a defence.

    4. Where necessary and practicable prisoners shall be allowed to make their defence through an interpreter.

37. Collective punishments, corporal punishment, punishment by

placing in a dark cell, and all cruel, inhuman or degrading punishment shall be completely prohibited as punishments for disciplinary offences.

38. 1. Punishment by disciplinary confinement and any other punishment which might have an adverse affect on the physical or mental health of the prisoner shall only be imposed if the medical officer, after examination, certifies in writing that the prisoner is fit to sustain it.

    2. In no case may such punishment be contrary to, or depart from the principles stated in Rule 37.

    3. The medical officer shall visit daily prisoners undergoing such punishment and shall advise the director if the termination or alteration of the punishment is considered necessary on grounds of physical or mental health.

INSTRUMENTS OF RESTRAINT

39. The use of chains and irons shall be prohibited. Handcuffs, restraint jackets and other body restraints shall never be applied as a punishment. They shall not be used except in the following circumstances:

    a. if necessary, as a precaution against escape during a transfer, provided that they shall be removed when the prisoner appears before a judicial or administrative authority unless that authority decides otherwise;

    b. on medical grounds by direction and under the supervision of the medical officer;

    c. by order of the director, if other methods of control fail, in order to protect a prisoner from self-injury, injury to others or to prevent serious damage to property; in such instances the director shall at once consult the medical officer and report to the higher administrative authority.

40. The patterns and manner of use of the instruments of restraint authorised in the preceding paragraph shall be decided by law or regulation. Such instruments must not be applied for any longer time than is strictly necessary.

INFORMATION TO AND COMPLAINTS BY PRISONERS

41. 1. Every prisoner shall on admission be provided with written information about the regulations governing the treatment of prisoners of the relevant category, the disciplinary requirements of the institution, the authorised methods of seeking information and making complaints, and all such other matters as are necessary to understand the rights and obligations of prisoners and to adapt to the life of the institution.

2. If a prisoner cannot understand the written information provided, this information shall be explained orally.

42. 1. Every prisoner shall have the opportunity every day of making   requests or complaints to the director of the institution or the officer authorised to act in that capacity.

2. A prisoner shall have the opportunity to talk to, or to make requests or complaints to, an inspector of prisons or to any other duly constituted authority entitled to visit the prison without the director or other members of staff being present. However, appeals against formal decisions may be restricted to the authorised procedures.

3. Every prisoner shall be allowed to make a request or complaint,   under confidential cover, to the central prison administration, the judicial authority or other proper authorities.

4. Every request or complaint addressed or referred to a prison authority shall be promptly dealt with and replied to by this authority without undue delay.

CONTACT WITH THE OUTSIDE WORLD

43. 1. Prisoners shall be allowed to communicate with their families and, subject to the needs of treatment, security and good order, persons or representatives of outside organisations and to receive visits from these persons as often as possible.

2. To encourage contact with the outside world there shall be a system of prison leave consistent with the treatment objectives in Part IV of these rules.

44. 1. Prisoners who are foreign nationals should be informed, without delay, of their right to request contact and be allowed reasonable facilities to communicate with the diplomatic or consular representative of the state to which they belong. The prison administrator should co-operate fully with such representatives in the interest of foreign nationals in prisons who may have special needs.

2. Prisoners who are nationals of states without diplomatic or consular representation in the country and refugees or stateless persons shall be allowed similar facilities to communicate with the diplomatic representative of the state which takes charge of their interests or national or international authority whose task it is to serve the interests of such persons.

45. Prisoners shall be allowed to keep themselves informed regularly of the news by reading newspapers, periodicals or other publications, by radio or television transmissions, by lectures or by any similar means as authorised or controlled by the administration. Special arrangements should be made to meet the needs of foreign nationals with linguistic difficulties.

RELIGIOUS AND MORAL ASSISTANCE

46. So far as practicable, every prisoner shall be allowed to satisfy the needs of his religious, spiritual and moral life by attending the services or meetings provided in the institution and having in his possession any necessary books or literature.

47. 1. If the institution contains a sufficient number of prisoners of the same religion, a qualified representative of that religion shall be appointed and approved. If the number of prisoners justifies it and conditions permit, the arrangement should be on a full-time basis.

2. A qualified representative appointed or approved under paragraph 1 shall be allowed to hold regular services and

activities and to pay pastoral visits in private to prisoners of his religion at proper times.

3. Access to a qualified representative of any religion shall not be refused to any prisoner. If any prisoner should object to a visit of any religious representative, the prisoner shall be allowed to refuse it.

RETENTION OF PRISONERS' PROPERTY

48. 1.   All money, valuables, and other effects belonging to prisoners which under the regulations of the institution they are not allowed to retain shall on admission to the institution be placed in safe custody. An inventory thereof shall be signed by the prisoner. Steps shall be taken to keep them in good condition. If it has been found necessary to destroy any article, this shall be recorded and the prisoner informed.

2. On the release of the prisoner, all such articles and money shall be returned except insofar as there have been authorised withdrawals of money or the authorised sending of any such property out of the institution, or it has been found necessary on hygienic grounds to destroy any article. The prisoner shall sign a receipt for the articles and money returned.

3. As far as practicable, any money or effects received for a prisoner from outside shall be treated in the same way unless they are intended for and permitted for use during imprisonment.

4. If a prisoner brings in any medicines, the medical officer shall decide what use shall be made of them.

NOTIFICATION OF DEATH, ILLNESS, TRANSFER, ETC.

49. 1.   Upon the death or serious illness of or serious injury to a prisoner, or removal to an institution for the treatment of mental illness or abnormalities, the director shall at once inform the spouse, if the prisoner is married, or the nearest relative and shall in any event inform any other person previously designated by the prisoner.

2. A prisoner shall be informed at once of the death or serious illness of any near relative. In these cases and whenever circumstances allow, the prisoner should be authorised to visit this sick relative or see the deceased either under escort or alone.

3. All prisoners shall have the right to inform at once their families of imprisonment or transfer to another institution.

REMOVAL OF PRISONERS

50. 1. When prisoners are being removed to or from an institution, they shall be exposed to public view as little as possible, and proper safeguards shall be adopted to protect them from insult, curiosity and publicity in any form.

2. The transport of prisoners in conveyances with inadequate ventilation or light, or in any way which would subject them to unnecessary physical hardship or indignity shall be prohibited.

3. The transport of prisoners shall be carried out at the expense of the administration and in accordance with duly authorised regulations.

Part III

PERSONNEL

51. In view of the fundamental importance of the prison staffs to the proper management of the institutions and the pursuit of their organisational and treatment objectives, prison administrations shall give high priority to the fulfilment of the rules concerning personnel.

52. Prison staff shall be continually encouraged through training, consultative procedures and a positive management style to aspire to humane standards, higher efficiency and a committed approach to their duties.

53. The prison administration shall regard it as an important task continually to inform public opinion of the roles of the prison system and the work of the staff, so as to encourage public understanding of the importance of their contribution to society.

54. 1. The prison administration shall provide for the careful selection on recruitment or in subsequent appointments of all personnel. Special emphasis shall be given to their integrity, humanity, professional capacity and personal suitability for the work.

    2. Personnel shall normally be appointed on a permanent basis as professional prison staff and have civil service status with security of tenure subject only to good conduct, efficiency, good physical and mental health and an adequate standard of education. Salaries shall be adequate to attract and retain suitable men and women; employment benefits and conditions of service shall be favourable in view of the exacting nature of the work.

    3. Whenever it is necessary to employ part-time staff, these criteria should apply to them as far as that is appropriate.

55. 1. On recruitment or after an appropriate period of practical experience, the personnel shall be given a course of training in their general and specific duties and be required to pass theoretical and practical tests unless their professional qualifications make that unnecessary.

    2. During their career, all personnel shall maintain and improve their knowledge and professional capacity by attending courses of in-service training to be organised by the administration at suitable intervals.

    3. Arrangements should be made for wider experience and training for personnel whose professional capacity would be improved by this.

    4. The training of all personnel should include instruction in the requirements and application of the European Prison Rules and the European Convention on Human Rights.

56. All members of the personnel shall be expected at all times so to conduct themselves and perform their duties as to influence the prisoners for their good by their example and to command their respect.

57. 1. So far as possible the personnel shall include a sufficient number of specialists such as psychiatrists, psychologists, social workers, teachers, trade, physical education and sports instructors.

    2. These and other specialist staff shall normally be employed on a permanent basis. This shall not preclude part-time or voluntary workers when that is appropriate and beneficial to the level of support and training they can provide.

58. 1. The prison administration shall ensure that every institution is at all times in the full charge of the director, the deputy director or other authorised official.

    2. The director of an institution should be adequately qualified for that post by character, administrative ability, suitable professional training and experience.

    3. The director shall be appointed on a full-time basis and be available or accessible as required by the prison administration in its management instructions.

    4. When two or more institutions are under the authority of one director, each shall be visited at frequent intervals. A responsible official shall be in charge of each of these institutions.

59. The administration shall introduce forms of organisation and management systems to facilitate communication between the different categories of staff in an institution with a view to ensuring co-operation between the various services, in particular, with respect to the treatment and re-socialisation of prisoners.

60. 1.   The director deputy, and the majority of other personnel of the institution shall be able to speak the language of the greatest number of prisoners, or a language understood by the greatest number of them.

  2.   Whenever necessary and practicable the services of an interpreter shall be used.

61. 1.   Arrangements shall be made to ensure at all times that a qualified and approved medical practitioner is able to attend without delay in cases of urgency.

  2.   In institutions not staffed by one or more full-time medical officers, a part-time medical officer or authorised staff of a health service shall visit regularly.

62. The appointment of staff in institutions or parts of institutions housing prisoners of the opposite sex is to be encouraged.

63. 1.   Staff of the institutions shall not use force against prisoners except in self-defence or in cases of attempted escape or active or passive physical resistance to an order based on law or regulations. Staff who have recourse to force must use no more than is strictly necessary and must report the incident immediately to the director of the institution.

  2.   Staff shall as appropriate be given special technical training to enable them to restrain aggressive prisoners.

  3.   Except in special circumstances, staff performing duties which bring them into direct contact with prisoners should not be armed. Furthermore, staff should in no circumstances be provided with arms unless they have been fully trained in their use.

Part IV

TREATMENT OBJECTIVES AND REGIMES

64. Imprisonment is by the deprivation of liberty a punishment in itself. The conditions of imprisonment and the prison regimes shall not, therefore, except as incidental to justifiable segregation

or the maintenance of discipline, aggravate the suffering inherent in this.

65. Every effort shall be made to ensure that the regimes of the institutions are designed and managed so as:

    a. to ensure that the conditions of life are compatible with human dignity and acceptable standards in the community;

    b. to minimise the detrimental effects of imprisonment and the differences between prison life and life at liberty which tend to diminish the self respect or sense of personal responsibility of prisoners;

    c. to sustain and strengthen those links with relatives and the outside community that will promote the best interests of prisoners and their families;

    d. to provide opportunities for prisoners to develop skills and aptitudes that will improve their prospects of successful resettlement after release.

66. To those ends all the remedial, educational, moral, spiritual and other resources that are appropriate should be made available and utilised in accordance with the individual treatment needs of prisoners. Thus the regimes should include:

    a. spiritual support and guidance and opportunities for relevant work, vocational guidance and training, education, physical education, the development of social skills, counselling and group and recreational activities;

    b. arrangements to ensure that these activities are organised, so far as possible, to increase contacts with and opportunities within the outside community so as to enhance the prospects for social resettlement after release;

    c. procedures for establishing and reviewing individual treatment and training programmes for prisoners after full consultations among the relevant staff and with individual prisoners who should be involved in these as far as is practicable;

d. communications systems and a management style that will encourage appropriate and positive relationships between staff and prisoners that will improve the prospects for effective and supportive regimes and treatment programmes.

67. 1. Since the fulfilment of these objectives requires individualisation of treatment and, for this purpose, a flexible system of allocation, prisoners should be placed in separate institutions or units where each can receive the appropriate treatment and training.

2. The type, size, organisation and capacity of these institutions should be determined essentially by the nature of the treatment to be provided.

3. It is necessary to ensure that prisoners are located with due regard to security and control but such measures should be the minimum compatible with safety and comprehend the special needs of the prisoner. Every effort should be made to place prisoners in institutions that are open in character or provide ample opportunities for contacts with the outside community. In the case of foreign nationals, links with people of their own nationality in the outside community are to be regarded as especially important.

68. As soon as possible after admission and after a study of the personality of each prisoner with a sentence of suitable length, a programme of treatment in a suitable institution shall be prepared in the light of the knowledge obtained about individual needs, capacities and dispositions, especially proximity to relatives.

69. 1. Within the regimes, prisoners shall be given the opportunity to participate in activities of the institution likely to develop their sense of responsibility, self-reliance and to stimulate interest in their own treatment.

2. Efforts should be made to develop methods of encouraging co-operation with and the participation of the prisoners in their treatment. To this end prisoners shall be encouraged to assume, within the limits specified in Rule 34, responsibilities in certain sectors of the institution's activity.

70. 1. The preparation of prisoners for release should begin as soon as possible after reception in a penal institution. Thus, the treatment of prisoners should emphasise not their exclusion from the community but their continuing part in it. Community agencies and social workers should, therefore, be enlisted wherever possible to assist the staff of the institution in the task of social rehabilitation of the prisoners particularly maintaining and improving the relationships with their families, with other persons and with the social agencies. Steps should be taken to safeguard, to the maximum extent compatible with the law and the sentence, the rights relating to civil interests, social security rights and other social benefits of prisoners.

    2. Treatment programmes should include provision for prison leave which should also be granted to the greatest extent possible on medical, educational, occupational, family and other social grounds.

    3. Foreign nationals should not be excluded from the arrangements for prison leave solely on account of their nationality. Furthermore, every effort should be made to enable them to participate in regime activities together so as to alleviate their feelings of isolation.

WORK

71. 1. Prison work should be seen as a positive element in treatment, training and institutional management.

    2. Prisoners under sentence may be required to work, subject to their physical and mental fitness as determined by the medical officer.

    3. Sufficient work of a useful nature, or if appropriate other purposeful activities shall be provided to keep prisoners actively employed for a normal working day.

    4. So far as possible the work provided shall be such as will maintain or increase the prisoner's ability to earn a normal living after release.

5. Vocational training in useful trades shall be provided for prisoners able to profit thereby and especially for young prisoners.

6. Within the limits compatible with proper vocational selection and with the requirements of institutional administration and discipline, the prisoners shall be able to choose the type of employment in which they wish to participate.

72. 1. The organisation and methods of work in the institutions shall resemble as closely as possible those of similar work in the community so as to prepare prisoners for the conditions of normal occupational life. It should thus be relevant to contemporary working standards and techniques and organised to function within modern management systems and production processes.

2. Although the pursuit of financial profit from industries in the institutions can be valuable in raising standards and improving the quality and relevance of training, the interests of the prisoners and of their treatment must not be subordinated to that purpose.

73. 1. Work for prisoners shall be assured by the prison administration:

a. either on its own premises, workshops and farms; or

b. in co-operation with private contractors inside or outside the institution in which case the full normal wages for such shall be paid by the persons to whom the labour is supplied, account being taken of the output of the prisoners.

74. 1. Safety and health precautions for prisoners shall be similar to those that apply to workers outside.

2. Provision shall be made to indemnify prisoners against industrial injury, including occupational disease, on terms not less favourable than those extended by law to workers outside.

75. 1. The maximum daily and weekly working hours of the prisoners shall be fixed in conformity with local rules or custom in regard to the employment of free workmen.

2. Prisoners should have at least one rest-day a week and sufficient time for education and other activities required as part of their treatment and training for social resettlement.

76. 1. There shall be a system of equitable remuneration of the work of prisoners.

    2. Under the system prisoners shall be allowed to spend at least a part of their earnings on approved articles for their own use and to allocate a part of their earnings to their family or for other approved purposes.

    3. The system may also provide that a part of the earnings be set aside by the administration so as to constitute a savings fund to be handed over to the prisoner on release.

EDUCATION

77. A comprehensive education programme shall be arranged in every institution to provide opportunities for all prisoners to pursue at least some of their individual needs and aspirations. Such programmes should have as their objectives the improvement of the prospects for successful social resettlement, the morale and attitudes of prisoners and their self-respect.

78. Education should be regarded as a regime activity that attracts the same status and basic remuneration within the regime as work, provided that it takes place in normal working hours and is part of an authorised individual treatment programme.

79. Special attention should be given by prison administrations to the education of young prisoners, those of foreign origin or with particular cultural or ethnic needs.

80. Specific programmes of remedial education should be arranged for prisoners with special problems such as illiteracy or innumeracy.

81. So far as practicable, the education of prisoners shall:

    a. be integrated with the educational system of the country so that after their release they may continue their education without difficulty;

b.   take place in outside educational institutions.

82. Every institution shall have a library for the use of all categories of prisoners, adequately stocked with a wide range of both recreational and instructional books, and prisoners shall be encouraged to make full use of it. Wherever possible the prison library should be organised in co-operation with community library services.

PHYSICAL EDUCATION, EXERCISE, SPORT AND RECREATION

83. The prison regimes shall recognise the importance to physical and mental health of properly organised activities to ensure physical fitness, adequate exercise and recreational opportunities.

84. Thus a properly organised programme of physical education, sport and other recreational activity should be arranged within the framework and objectives of the treatment and training regime. To this end space, installations and equipment should be provided.

85. Prison administrations should ensure that prisoners who participate in these programmes are physically fit to do so. Special arrangements should be made, under medical direction, for remedial physical education and therapy for those prisoners who need it.

86. Every prisoner who is not employed in outdoor work, or located in an open institution, shall be allowed, if the weather permits, at least one hour of walking or suitable exercise in the open air daily, as far as possible, sheltered from inclement weather.

PRE-RELEASE PREPARATION

87. All prisoners should have the benefit of arrangements designed to assist them in returning to society, family life and employment after release. Procedures and special courses should be devised to this end.

88. In the case of those prisoners with longer sentences, steps should be taken to ensure a gradual return to life in society. This aim may be achieved, in particular, by a pre-release regime organised

in the same institution or in another appropriate institution, or by conditional releases under some kind of supervision combined with effective social support.

89. 1.   Prison administrations should work closely with the social services and agencies that assist released prisoners to re-establish themselves in society, in particular with regard to family life and employment.

2.   Steps must be taken to ensure that on release prisoners are provided, as necessary, with appropriate documents and identification papers, and assisted in finding suitable homes and work to go to. They should also be provided with immediate means of subsistence, be suitably and adequately clothed having regard to the climate and season, and have sufficient means to reach their destination.

3.   The approved representatives of the social agencies or services should be afforded all necessary access to the institution and to prisoners with a view to making a full contribution to the preparation for release and after-care programme of the prisoner.

Part V

ADDITIONAL RULES FOR SPECIAL CATEGORIES

90.   Prison administrations should be guided by the provisions of the rules as a whole as far as they can appropriately and in practice be applied for the benefit of those special categories of prisoners for which additional rules are provided hereafter.

UNTRIED PRISONERS

91.   Without prejudice to legal rules for the protection of individual liberty or prescribing the procedure to be observed in respect of untried prisoners, these prisoners, who are presumed to be innocent until they are found guilty, shall be afforded the benefits that may derive from Rule 90 and treated without restrictions other than those necessary for the penal procedure and the security of the institution.

92. 1. Untried prisoners shall be allowed to inform their families of their detention immediately and given all reasonable facilities for communication with family and friends and persons with whom it is in their legitimate interest to enter into contact.

2. They shall also be allowed to receive visits from them under humane conditions subject only to such restrictions and supervision as are necessary in the interests of the administration of justice and of the security and good order of the institution.

3. If an untried prisoner does not wish to inform any of these persons, the prison administration should not do so on its own initiative unless there are good overriding reasons as, for instance, the age, state of mind or any other incapacity of the prisoner.

93. Untried prisoners shall be entitled, as soon as imprisoned, to choose a legal representative, or shall be allowed to apply for free legal aid where such aid is available and to receive visits from that legal adviser with a view to their defence and to prepare and hand to the legal adviser, and to receive confidential instructions. On request, they shall be given all necessary facilities for this purpose. In particular, they shall be given the free assistance of an interpreter for all essential contacts with the administration and for their defence. Interviews between prisoners and their legal advisers may be within sight but not within hearing, either direct or indirect, of the police or institution staff. The allocation of untried prisoners shall be in conformity with the provisions of Rule 11, paragraph 3.

94. Except where there are circumstances that make it undesirable, untried prisoners shall be given the opportunity of having separate rooms.

95. 1. Untried prisoners shall be given the opportunity of wearing their own clothing if it is clean and suitable.

2. Prisoners who do not avail themselves of this opportunity shall be supplied with suitable dress.

3. If they have no suitable clothing of their own, untried prisoners shall be provided with civilian clothing in good condition in which to appear in court or on authorised outings.

96. Untried prisoners shall, whenever possible, be offered the opportunity to work but shall not be required to work. Those who choose to work shall be paid as other prisoners. If educational or trade training is available, untried prisoners shall be encouraged to avail themselves of these opportunities.

97. Untried prisoners shall be allowed to procure at their own expense or at the expense of a third party such books, newspapers, writing materials and other means of occupation as are compatible with the interests of the administration of justice and the security and good order of the institution.

98. Untried prisoners shall be given the opportunity of being visited and treated by their own doctor or dentist if there is reasonable ground for the application. Reasons should be given if the application is refused. Such costs as are incurred shall not be the responsibility of the prison administration.

CIVIL PRISONERS

99. In countries where the law permits imprisonment by order of a court under any non-criminal process, persons so imprisoned shall not be subjected to any greater restriction or severity than is necessary to ensure safe custody and good order. Their treatment shall not be less favourable than that of untried prisoners, with the reservation, however, that they may be required to work.

INSANE AND MENTALLY ABNORMAL PRISONERS

100. 1. Persons who are found to be insane should not be detained in prisons and arrangements shall be made to remove them to appropriate establishments for the mentally ill as soon as possible.

2. Specialised institutions or sections under medical management should be available for the observation and treatment of prisoners suffering gravely from other mental disease or abnormality.

3. The medical or psychiatric service of the penal institutions shall provide for the psychiatric treatment of all prisoners who are in need of such treatment.

4. Action should be taken, by arrangement with the appropriate community agencies, to ensure where necessary the continuation of psychiatric treatment after release and the provision of social psychiatric after-care.

ANNEX D: INFORMATION SHEET 21:

PRISONER ADJUDICATION PROCEDURES

1.   You will receive this Information Sheet together with Form 1127 which informs you of the charge(s) against you. You should receive this Information Sheet and Form 1127 at least 2 hours before the adjudication.

2.   Where the offence is of a serious nature the Governor may refer the charge to the Secretary of State. In most cases the Secretary of State will delegate his authority to conduct the adjudication to the Board of Visitors or Visiting Committee. If your case is to be heard by members of the Board of Visitors or the Visiting Committee you will be informed.

3.   You may request to see a copy of all statements to be submitted in evidence and be informed of the names of any witnesses to the incident in advance of the hearing.

4.   You may, if you wish, seek to consult with a solicitor before the adjudication. If you are not able to consult your solicitor before the hearing the adjudicator will decide if it is necessary for the hearing to be adjourned to allow you to do so. If an adjournment is granted a date for the resumption of the hearing will be set. If you have not asked for or received advice by the time the adjudication is reconvened it may proceed. If you do not know of a solicitor who will act for you a list of solicitors will be made available to you on request.

The Adjudication

5.   The procedure at the adjudication is as follows. If at any stage of the proceedings you do not understand what is happening you should say so.

6.   To open the adjudication the adjudicator will:

   a)   ask if you have received Form 1127 and this Information Sheet and if you understand the adjudication procedures;

b) read out the charge and ask if you understand it - if the charge differs from that on Form 1127 or you are in any doubt about the charge you should say so;

c) ask if you have had sufficient time to prepare an answer to the charge - if you consider you need more time you should state your reasons so that the possibility of an adjournment may be considered;

d) ask if you would like the question of legal representation or other assistance to be considered - you will have to state your reasons for requesting legal representation or assistance and the decision on whether to grant your request will lie with the adjudicator;

e) ask, on each charge separately, whether you plead guilty or not guilty - if you make no plea you will be treated as having pleaded not guilty;

f) ask if you wish to call witnesses.

7. The reporting officer will give his or her evidence and you will then have the opportunity to question the officer on his or her statement.

8. If there are any witnesses in support of the charge(s) against you they will give their evidence and you will be allowed to question them. If you do not feel able to adequately put your question to a witness explain your point to the adjudicator who may assist you by asking questions on your behalf.

9. If you have pleaded guilty you may make a verbal statement including any factors you wish to be taken into consideration by the adjudicator in reaching a finding.

10. If you have pleaded not guilty you may now make your defence to the charge(s) laid. Any written statement you have made can be read and you may comment on the evidence given. You may also ask to call witnesses. You will need to tell the adjudicator what you think their evidence will prove and they will be called where the adjudicator is satisfied their evidence will assist in establishing exactly what happened. You will be able to question the witnesses on their evidence or any relevant matter

and they may also be questioned by others present including the reporting officer.

11. After your witnesses (if any) have been heard you may make a further statement if you wish.

12. The adjudicator may adjourn the adjudication at any stage of the proceedings where he or she finds it necessary and the reason for any adjournment will be explained to you.

13. In the case of a Governor's adjudication if, after hearing the evidence, he is satisfied that a lesser alternative charge would be more appropriate, he may substitute that for the original charge. If this happens you will be given the opportunity to respond to the new charge.

14. Having heard all the evidence the adjudicator will announce the findings on each charge.

15. If you are found guilty the adjudicator will ask you if there is anything that you wish to say in support of a request for leniency before any punishment is imposed. You may also ask to call someone, readily available, who may make such comments for you.

16. The adjudicator may ask for a report on your conduct in custody to be given and you will be able to ask questions in connection with that report.

17. The adjudicator will then announce the award(s) for any offence(s) proved. If you do not understand how you will be affected by the award(s) you should ask for it to be explained to you.

18. If you do not understand any of the points made in this information sheet or need any other information about the conduct of the hearing you should ask a member of prison staff to assist you.

19. It is in your interests to attend the adjudication. However you should be aware that if you refuse to attend the adjudication it may still take place in your absence. Once a finding has been made you will be given an opportunity to attend to make a plea

in mitigation. If you still refuse to attend you will be informed of the result of the hearing.

ANNEX E: CASES CITED

Becker v Home Office, [1972] 2 QB 407

Christofi v Home Office, [1975] *The Times* 31 July, 1975

Egerton v Home Office, [1978] Crim LR 494

Ferguson v Home Office, [1977] *The Times* 8 October, 1977

F.C. Shepherd & Co. v. Jerrom [1987] Q.B. 301.

Golder v UK, [1975] 1 EHRR 524 (European Court of Human Rights)

Hamer v UK [1982] 4 EHRR 139 (European Court).

Hare v. Murphy Bros [1974] 3 All ER 940

Hone v Board of Visitors, HM Prison Maze, [1988] 1 All ER 321

In re Crockard's Application, [1985] 13 NIJB 69

In re Duffin's Application, CA [1988] 21 December 1988

In re Hardy's Application, [1988] 12 NIJB 66

In re Hunter's Application, [1989] 1 NIJB 86

In re Mulvenna's Application [1985] 13 NIJB 76

In re Murphy's Application, [1988] 8 NIJB 94

In re O'Hare's Application, [1988] 2 NIJB 56

In re Quinn's Application, [1988] 5 BNIL 107

In re Stephenson's Application, CA [1987] 4 NIJB 57

Meddleweek v Chief Constable of Merseyside, CA [1985] *The Times* 1 August, 1985

Porterfield v Home Office, [1988] *The Times* 9 March, 1988.

Raymond v Honey, [1982] 1 All ER 756

R v Board of Visitors, HM Prison Blundeston, ex parte Fox-Taylor, [1982] 1 All ER 646

R v Board of Visitors, HM Prison Gartree, ex parte Mealy, [1981] *The Times*

14 November 1981

R v Board of Visitors, HM Prison Hull, ex parte St Germain (No 2), [1979] 3 All ER 545

R v Deputy Governor of Parkhurst Prison, ex parte Hague, CA 25 May, 1990

R v Home Secretary, ex parte Anderson, [1984] 1 All ER 920

R v Home Secretary ex parte Leech [1993] 4 ALL ER 539

R v Home Secretary, ex parte Tarrant, [1984] 1 All ER 799

Robb v Secretary of State [1995] 1 ALL ER 677

Spence v NIO [1993] NILR 97

Steele v NIO [1989] 1 NIJB 120

W v Edgell [1990] Ch 359

Williams v Home Office, [1981] 1 All ER 1151

INDEX

Please note: This index does not cover the Annexes